Five Timelines

Five Timelines:

Modern Israel
and
Old Testament Prophecy

by
Mike Lester

For Mary,

My biggest fan,

"She openeth her mouth with wisdom;
and in her tongue is the law of kindness."

Proverbs 31:26

Contents

Preface

In late 2023, I finally decided to move ahead and independently publish my book, *2520: The Hidden Key in the Book of Daniel.* I had been rejected by multiple publishers and reached a point where I realized that, if I wanted the book to be published, I would have to do it myself. By early 2024, the first copies were available on Amazon.com.

During the year that followed, I spoke to a couple of churches, sharing my thoughts about the book. I handed out free signed copies, answered questions, delivered presentations, and refined my arguments in various ways. Nothing will help you learn a topic quite as much as trying to teach it to others.

During that year, I compiled research from other parts of the Bible. The number 2,520 occurs elsewhere in scripture, embedded into the text and narratives of the Bible in various ways. Most of these occurrences do not seem to have prophetic implications. Though I am not sure about this, it appears as though some of the Old Testament authors used these embedded equations as a sort of 'checksum' in order to ensure the documents were accurately copied by scribes.

I brought my research together into a larger work, which I was going to title, *"2,520: A Timeline For Our Times."* It was not a particularly difficult task, other than dealing with the size of the undertaking. The research was completed; I only needed to organize it into an understandable format.

While working on that larger project, I came across modern Israel's Declaration of Establishment. I had never read the Declaration before, though from the standpoint of Old Testament prophecy, it was arguably the most momentous document of the 20th century.

The creation of modern Israel in 1948 was a seismic event in Middle Eastern and international politics. From the moment of her creation and independence, Israel's existence has been a challenge for diplomats and politicians who have tried to balance historical claims to the land with modern geopolitical realities.

Interpreters of scripture were shaken by the creation of Israel as well. Suddenly, the Old Testament verses predicting a return of the Jewish people to their homeland had to be examined literally, rather than allegorically.

The creation of modern Israel united the modern Muslim world in a way that it had not been united in centuries. Muslims around the world rallied behind the belief that Al Aqsa Mosque on the Temple Mount must not be lost to infidel control. This emotional rationale bound Muslims to the fate of Jerusalem. Even today, any perceived threat to the Temple Mount by Israel or anyone else, results in protests from Palestinian Arabs and Muslim diplomats worldwide.

The creation of Israel was a seismic event for Christians too. Christians suddenly had to reevaluate their understanding of Old Testament prophecy. For centuries, many Christians interpreted the biblical prediction of a Jewish return to Palestine as already fulfilled. They often reinterpreted those verses as metaphors or allegories meant for the Church herself. Suddenly, a literalist view of the Old Testament demanded reconsideration.

I was surprised by what I found in Israel's Declaration of Establishment. I had expected to find Israel's moral justification for its creation. I had expected to find the Jewish vision for the establishment of Israel and its place in the world. What I did not expect to find were references to historical events connected to specific scriptures by timelines of 2,520 years.

What caught my eye when I read the Declaration of Establishment were references to five modern historical events. Each of these events could be dated and was connected to Old Testament verses by embedded timelines which I had already identified in my research.

I was both shocked and encouraged by this discovery. I was shocked that the Declaration contained these references, and encouraged that I had a hook to begin another book.

I began writing a new book immediately, averaging about 2,000 words a day. All the research had already been completed over a period of more than three years, so the project moved quickly. All I had to do was organize my thoughts and put them on paper in a way that others could understand. I completed the initial draft in three-and-a-half weeks.

In addition—or in parallel to this book, I wrote five essays detailing my findings and submitted them for copyright registration. Those five essays became the foundation for the five primary chapters of this book. For that three-week period, virtually nothing else mattered to me; even my daughter's wedding was a faraway thought compared to this project.

I finished the first draft four days before my daughter's wedding. I set it aside for a few days to enjoy the company of friends and family while celebrating my daughter's next stage in life. The book could wait.

After decompressing from the wedding, I returned to the book and began the edits. The edits took as long as writing the book.

What you will read in these pages is the product of more than three years of research, but it is a very small part of what I have uncovered. I have condensed my findings into the most salient and impactful verses connected to the establishment of Israel and the embedded timelines related to the Declaration of Establishment.

The average person might think of these timelines as codes. The embedded numbers and their intended equations are hidden from view and understanding in a way that is reminiscent of codes and enciphered messages. What I will demonstrate in this book is technically neither a code nor a cipher. The technical term is steganography.

Steganography is a method of embedding or hiding a secret message or key within an existing message. For instance, a person might write a love letter that, to all appearances, is just a personal message. However, if we discover invisible ink on the same letter, it becomes much more than its apparent intent. Spies during World War II sometimes hid extremely tiny messages in microdot films the size of a period. Those microdots could be affixed to a postcard or an envelope and escape the notice of secret police. In each of these cases, the legitimate overt message can be read and understood, but hidden within the message itself or its container is another 'secret' message.

These embedded equations in the Bible were missed in the past, because we did not know to search for them. Like the microdot film affixed to a letter, we overlooked them because they were hidden in the larger, more obvious message.

These embedded equations do not diminish the primary scripture or its meaning. They do not refute what is written; instead, they seem to add to the scripture. In certain cases, they offer evidence that the scripture has remained unchanged for thousands of years despite being copied multiple times. In other cases, we have evidence that the scripture was written with a divine intent.

As a result of my research into these numbers, I have arrived at a couple of conclusions. First, the Bible is the product of a supernatural intelligence; these scriptures were written by men but superintended by God. Second, modern Israel exists because God wants Israel to exist.

Those are extraordinary claims. To claim that any document was created by God, is an extraordinary claim. Likewise, it is an extravagantly bold assertion to claim that Israel exists because God wants her to exist. I provide evidence for those claims in the next 100 or so pages of this book.

Acknowledgments

Much of the research for this book relied heavily on certain online resources.

Blue Letter Bible at blueletterbible.com was instrumental to my research. Their website is easy to use, contains a wide variety of language tools, and offers the ability to do string searches in the original language. They are worthy of your monetary support and donations.

CSGNetwork.com contains a large number of tools for calculating dates, and days between dates. Accurately determining the timelines in this book would not have been possible without their Julian Date Calculator.

The Babylonian math calculations were done with the help of the Babylonian numbers conversion tool on the dCode.fr website. DCode has a wide variety of cryptographic and math tools that are useful for anyone who is interested in ancient math systems or older cryptographic techniques.

Jewishvirtuallibrary.org was also a very helpful reference for specific events in modern Jewish history and brief biographical sketches.

While I used several online sources for biographical background on Theodor Herzl, the most entertaining and enlightening source that I found was *Herzl*, by Shlomo Avineri. Avineri tells Herzl's story in a way that is both entertaining and informative. If you enjoy history, or an entertaining biography, please, let me recommend *Herzl*.

I'd like to thank my friend Randy Pace for offering his time and resources to provide the author's photograph.

My wife continues to support me and shows faith in me even in moments when I doubt myself. She is my greatest encouragement.

Finally, nothing that I have written or learned would have been possible without God. He is the source of all wisdom, knowledge, and understanding. The strength, motivation and insight that it took to write this book came from Him.

Introduction

My Promises to the Reader

In this book, you will find incontrovertible evidence—as plain as printed text—that the Bible has a supernatural origin. I will show you timelines that have been embedded in the text of the Bible for 25 centuries, unseen and unrevealed. These timelines connect prophecies in the Old Testament to the history of modern Israel.

After you finish this book, you will never look at the Bible in quite the same way. You will never look at modern Israel in quite the same way again. That is my promise to you, the reader.

Some of what I demonstrate in this book may be difficult to understand at first. Some of these concepts may seem foreign. The men who wrote the Old Testament lived a long time ago. They had different ways of understanding the world, different math systems, different languages, different calendars, and different dating systems. There is a lot to learn. I will make it as simple as I can. That is my promise.

A Miraculous Nation

On May 14, 1948, modern Israel declared her independence when 37 representatives of the Israeli provisional government gathered to sign the Declaration of Establishment of the State of Israel. This document, consisting of about eighteen paragraphs,[1] expresses the core justifications for the existence of Israel.

The Declaration outlines the various claims of the Jewish people to the land of Israel. They base these claims on heritage, history, religion, and international agreement. The Jewish people's earliest history establishes their connection to the land. Their claim is spiritual because they were chosen by God to occupy the land; they were also chosen to write and protect the Old Testament of the Holy Bible. Their claim is political and legal because the United Nations had declared their right to settle in Mandatory Palestine.

The signing of the Declaration was a seismic moment in world history. Israel had not existed as an independent state for 2,000 years.

---

[1] See Appendix I for a full English Translation

The Romans destroyed Jerusalem in AD 70, and then again in AD 135, scattering the Jewish people across the Middle East and Europe. In the history of the world, no other nation—so long dead and scattered—has been resurrected in this manner.

The Bible, through the Old Testament prophets, foretold this national rebirth. The prophets predicted that the people, though scattered, would one day return. The same God who chose Abraham, who chose Moses, and who brought the Israelites out of Egypt, would gather them again to the land He had promised. In 1948, those prophecies seemed to be unfolding.

Though Old Testament prophets predicted a future 'gathering together' of the Jewish people and the resurrection of the Jewish state, few believed it. In many Christian circles, the common custom was to treat those passages of the Old Testament in one of three ways: they were ignored, they were dismissed as already fulfilled in 538 BC,[2] or they were allegorized into meaninglessness.

Those who allegorized the Old Testament prophecies asserted that these passages were a picture of the believer's struggle with sin and his relationship with God or that these were allegories of God's dealings with the Church. A common belief was that the Church had replaced Israel in prophecy, making it difficult for Christians to take predictions of a literal return seriously.

From a certain perspective, it seems reasonable to have doubted the predictions of a future Jewish state in Palestine. Centuries had passed since the Jewish people were first scattered across the globe. In most places, they were subject to persecution and oppression. Even though they continued to maintain their religious and cultural identity, they seemed to be the weakest of peoples.

At the end of World War II, in 1945, the Jewish people appeared to be at their absolute weakest. The promises of a return to Palestine and a national home seemed like the most absurd of impossibilities. Yet by 1948, Jewish communities around the world nervously celebrated the establishment of a Jewish homeland in Palestine. The impossible had happened—but could it last?

---

[2] The book of Ezra chronicles the return of the Jewish people to Jerusalem, beginning with the decree of Cyrus the Great in 538 BC.

Once the Declaration was signed, five Arab states declared war and invaded the fledgling nation. With invaders on all sides, a Jewish victory seemed impossible. The infant nation shocked the world, however. By mid-1949, all the invading Arab states, except one, had signed armistice agreements. The impossible had happened, Israel was reborn and had survived its first war.

So, perhaps the Old Testament prophecies could be understood literally, after all? After 2,000 years, the Old Testament prophecies of a return were relevant. All their predictions of a national resurrection and a return from the wilderness of the nations were no longer difficult portions of scripture to be allegorized or dismissed. Conservative interpretations of scripture and so-called 'literalists' had to be considered seriously again.

Can We Take the Bible Seriously?

Ultimately, when it comes to the Bible, that is the real question, isn't it? Can we really take the Bible literally? Should we take the prophecies seriously? What reason do we have to believe these passages of scripture are anything more than just dusty old stories and bits of religious wisdom?

The claims of Judaism and Christianity rest on the completely radical and outrageous proposition that the Bible exists as a communication from God. Beyond that, Judaism and Christianity contend that humanity is accountable for the truths contained in this supernatural communication.

As radical as these propositions are, they are either true or false. Either the Bible is supernatural in origin and motive, or it is no more important than any other ancient literature. The proposition that the Bible is the word of God demands evidence. Any freethinking person would expect evidence to be presented before they would willingly trust themselves to such a proposition.

The only evidence that could validate the supernatural origin of scripture would be supernatural evidence. In the Bible, miracles support the divine authority of the prophet and reinforce the moral message that he delivers. Supernatural evidence, the miracle, supports the claim that the messenger is sent by God, and the message is from God.

The only miracle I know of that a printed text can provide is miraculous prediction. I am referring to prophecy—a miraculous prediction that is fulfilled. Prophecy consists of a moral message accompanied by a miraculous prediction. When such a prediction is fulfilled, this affirms the authority of the prophet and the divine origin of the moral message.

Defining What Constitutes Proof

So, what would constitute proof that the scriptures predicting a return to the land, or a national resurrection were accurate? In other words, how do we know that the 'fulfilled' prophecies about Israel weren't just a coincidence? What would serve as evidence that all these dusty, cryptic passages were connected to the 20th century AD?

Realistically, any confirmation would require specificity. The connection would have to be unmistakable—as plain as black ink on a white page. The connection would have to be easy to understand. Yet, the connection would have to be so incomprehensibly mysterious that the evidence points to something that is unexplainable by nature or natural means.

In the 20th century, our critical, scientific age demands proofs that are objective, measurable, and independently verifiable. Numbers—we adore them. Numbers to measure, to evaluate, to criticize, to confirm, and to compare. Ultimately, a truly accurate prophecy about the future would establish a fixed timeline, connecting dates that could be independently confirmed or refuted.

The timeline or date could not be too obvious, however. If the date or the timeline were stated plainly, then people might try to fulfill the prophecy through artificial means. If the prophecy happened because human beings knowingly orchestrated and manipulated events, then it would not be a miracle, it would be a human creation.

The Universe's Double-blind Experiment

What we need then, is a sort of double-blind experiment. Once the events have occurred, the sealed files would be opened to examine the data. Neither the observer nor the subjects would have prior knowledge of the dates or timelines before the study's conclusion. That would provide the proof.

First, a historic event would have to take place that is connected, literally or figuratively, to an Old Testament prophecy. The prophecy itself must be datable. Either the prophecy must be associated with an event that can be dated, or the prophet names the date of the prophecy. Somewhere in the prophecy we would discover a timeline connecting the words of the prophet to the historic event. The timeline must, with reasonable accuracy, connect the date of the prophecy to the date of the historic event.

None of this could be easily recognizable before the events occurred; otherwise, people would try to make the prophecy come true themselves. It would need to be revealed after the fact.

There would have to be multiple occurrences of this phenomenon; a single instance could not be considered any more than coincidence.

My Promise to the Reader

This is my promise to the reader, as I said before: in this book, you will find incontrovertible evidence—clear and unmistakable—that the Bible has a supernatural origin. I will show you timelines that have been embedded in the text of the Bible for 25 centuries, unseen and unrevealed. What I will show relies on numbers, numbers you can see, count, add, and multiply. I promise these numbers are easy to understand.

These numbers were meant to be understood as timelines. These timelines connect dates in the Bible to historic events in the 19th and 20th century AD. Here's the kicker: every one of these modern events is mentioned in the Declaration of Establishment of the State of Israel. Each of the Old Testament prophecies contains parallels to the 19th and 20th-century events. I promise to show the parallels.

In short, what I will show in the Bible is at once, easy to understand, yet still so incomprehensibly mysterious as to defy natural explanation. In other words, after reading this book I think you will conclude that the Bible contains information from a source that is, by definition, supernatural.

There is a supernatural intelligence behind what is written in the Bible. That is my outrageous claim; I promise to present evidence supporting that claim.

Daniel and Jeremiah claimed that their revelations came from God. This book presents evidence that that is true. Yet, that is not the only thing that I will show you in this book.

These timelines provide evidence—hard, objective, measurable, and independently verifiable evidence—linking the prophecies of Daniel and Jeremiah to modern Israel. So, my other promise to the reader is this, when you finish this book, you will have seen convincing evidence that the modern state of Israel is of particular interest to God. God cares a lot about Israel.

I have one warning: when you have finished this book, you will not be able to look at the Bible or modern Israel in quite the same way. For some people, what I write will confirm what they already believe. Other people may be disturbed or angered by what I propose.

Public opinion supporting Israel in the United States is still strong, but the opposition to Israel seems to be the strongest that it has ever been. The voices of hatred on American campuses may be a relatively small number, but they are loud. In the past several years, we have seen demonstrators change their slogans from, "Palestinian lives matter," to, "Death to Israel," and "Death to the Jews." If you are sympathetic to those voices, what I write here may leave you unsettled or even angry.

Buckle up. Enjoy the ride.

Chapter One

Understanding the Equations

No Special Skills Required

There is nothing magical or mysterious in any of these embedded equations. None of this analysis requires an advanced college degree or a seminary education. All of the numbers are based on the original languages of the Bible. I used online software to assist me in my analysis. While it might be helpful to be able to read Hebrew or Aramaic, you don't need a knowledge of any foreign language to understand these equations. Most of the numbers (about 80%) that I show in this book can be easily confirmed by using a King James Bible.

Why the King James Version?

The King James Bible was written about 400 years ago and was translated by men who tried to capture the original meaning and original words in the Bible and transfer them directly into English. I say transfer, because generally speaking, if they read a particular noun or verb in the original language, they transferred that into English as closely as they could to the original language. As a result, nouns in the original languages (Hebrew and Aramaic) tend to occur the same number of times in the English of the King James Version. They do not transfer 100% of the time this way, but it works well enough that you can confirm most of my work without using online tools.

Please do not misunderstand me. I am not arguing that the King James Version of the Bible is a 'superior' translation or that it is the 'best' translation. I have simply found that it works best for what I am trying to demonstrate in this book. As the saying goes, "It's the best tool for the job"—for this particular job.

As to which translations are "best," I leave that argument to people who are much more qualified to judge than I am. I have experience translating and interpreting foreign languages, but I don't know the languages of the Bible well enough to offer an educated evaluation. For the sake of this book, it is enough to recognize the difference between verbs and nouns and to be able to count. The arguments about, "best" translations and "superior" manuscripts are topics best left for someone else's book.

Assigning Values to Nouns and Verbs—Detecting the Equations

When reading the Bible, you may have noticed how repetitive some of the language is. The authors of the Bible often used a literary structure known as parallelism to construct their stories and narratives. Parallelism uses repetitive themes or ideas to create a familiar structure that is easy to understand and often easy to memorize. Some examples of parallel structures in literature are:

- "Black is white and white is black." Kevin Costner in Oliver Stone's *JFK,* 1991.
- "fair is foul and foul is fair." Shakespeare, *Macbeth,* Act One, Scene One.
- "Let us never negotiate out of fear but let us never fear to negotiate." John F. Kennedy, Inaugural Address, 1961.
- Pride goeth before destruction, and an haughty spirit before a fall. Proverbs 16:18

The Bible frequently uses parallel structures. As a result, many of the stories may seem repetitive. A natural consequence of this repetition is frequent use of certain words in a story. For instance, in Daniel 2, the word 'king' occurs 48 times in the original languages—48! Even for the Bible, that's quite repetitive. In fact, it's so repetitive that some English translations reduce the total count to avoid redundancy. For example, the NIV uses the word 'king' only 37 times.[3]

Now, lots of people have noticed that numbers in the Bible are meaningful. Volumes have been written about the spiritual or esoteric meaning of different numbers in the Bible. It is no surprise then, that the frequency of word occurrences in the Bible is intentional and meaningful. For example, Sodom and Gomorrah occur together in Genesis a total of nine times. Nine is a number that represents judgment; those cities were famous for the fact that God judged them. Similarly, the word 'flood' occurs nine times in the biographical

---

[3] I use single quotations to refer to the word in terms of what it means. The Hebrew and Aramaic word *melek,* is *'king'* in English. Double quotations represent the words as they appear in the English translation of the Bible.

account of Noah in Genesis; God judged the earth in Noah's lifetime by sending a flood.[4]

In the creation story, God created the world with 10 commands. Later he gave the Ten Commandments to Moses as a moral law around which the Hebrews were to structure their lives and society. It is evident that numbers hold significance in scripture.

None of what I have written so far about numbers in the Bible is new or surprising. However, there appears to be an aspect to these numbers that people have missed. Believe it or not, after literally thousands of years of reading and studying the Bible, people missed something kind of unique and interesting about the numbers in the Bible. Sometimes those numbers can be combined to form interesting equations. What makes these equations intriguing is that certain sums and products occur more commonly than others.

One of the more common products and, in certain ways, more interesting, is the number 2,520. This number occurs with surprising frequency embedded in some parts of the Bible. The number 2,520 is never there in a particularly obvious way, but it is hidden in subtle ways in the narrative or the structure.

In addition to 2,520, the number 42 appears frequently. Interestingly, 2,520 is the product of 42 and 60, making these numbers, in a sense, like relatives. Remarkably, the ancient Babylonians even wrote the numbers 2,520 and 42 in the exact same way—no kidding! You'll learn more about this in the next chapter, where, unfortunately, there will be math. Sorry.

There are other 'cousins' of 2,520 that occur in scripture, 252 (one tenth of 2,520), 1,260 (one-half of 2,520), and, in more than one place, 907,200 (2,520 times 360).

For the sake of this book, we will only focus on relatively easy-to-spot occurrences of 2,520. Each of the prophecies reviewed in this book contains the number 2,520 embedded in the text. Additionally, each of these prophecies is also connected to the history of the

---

[4] The word flood occurs a total of 12 times in Genesis overall, but 9 times in the passages discussing Noah's life. Twelve is symbolically significant number in the Bible.

Jewish people or to the modern state of Israel by timelines of 2,520 years.[5]

None of these prophetic timelines connect to Gentile nations. There are no connections to 9/11, Napolean, JFK, Donald Trump, Merovingian kings, modern Christian 'prophets,' or ancient alien astronauts. The only connection to Gentiles is in how they influence the Jewish people or the modern state of Israel.

It turns out that the Bible—while written by human beings— was inspired and superintended by an intelligence that is intensely interested in the Jewish people, Jerusalem, and the state of Israel. When the Bible says things like—Israel is the apple of God's eye—it means Israel.

Discrete Values Relate to Noun Frequency and Cardinal Numbers

These numbers have been embedded in the text and stories of the Bible in various ways. In this book, I focus primarily on noun frequency. It's pretty simple: a noun is assigned a discrete numerical value based on its frequency of occurrence in a story or chapter of the Bible. I will show how these nouns were combined in sentences so that, if they are multiplied together, they equal 2,520 or 907,200. No kidding—these numbers really occur.

Sometimes, the numbers are sitting there right in the text as either cardinal numbers (one, two, three, etc.) or as ordinal numbers (first, second, third, etc.). The numbers can be added or multiplied with one another. More often, however, the stated numbers are multiplied by the discrete noun frequency values.

The awesome part of this is that you don't need any special knowledge or education to see these numbers. Simple, middle school-level multiplication or primary school addition is all it takes. You can count the numbers on your fingers or perform the calculations using even the most basic calculator.

---

[5] On occasion these are 2,520 modified years of 360 days. I will discuss this concept in chapter three.

Let's look at a couple of examples. It's always better to show than explain, anyway. So, observe the next couple of examples and then we will dig into the rest of the book.

2520 in Exodus 15

> *So, Moses brought Israel from the Red sea, and they went out into the wilderness of Shur; and they went* **three days** *in the wilderness, and found no water. And when they came to Marah, they could not drink of the waters of Marah, for they were bitter: therefore the name of it was called Marah. And the people murmured against Moses, saying, What shall we drink? And he cried unto the LORD; and the LORD shewed him a tree, which when he had cast into the waters, the waters were made sweet: there he made for them a statute and an ordinance, and there he proved them, And said, If thou wilt diligently hearken to the voice of the LORD thy God, and wilt do that which is right in his sight, and wilt give ear to his commandments, and keep all his statutes, I will put none of these diseases upon thee, which I have brought upon the Egyptians: for I am the LORD that healeth thee. And they came to Elim, where were* **twelve wells of water,** *and* **threescore and ten palm trees:** *and they encamped there by the waters. Exodus 15:22-27 (Boldface added)*

Exodus, the second book of Moses, recounts the events of Moses' life leading up to and including his leadership in freeing the Hebrew slaves from captivity. Exodus contains at least one passage where the embedded numbers result in a product of 2,520. This brief story in Exodus 15:22-27 describes the children of Israel in the wilderness. It contains three cardinal numbers in the narrative. The Israelites traveled for **three days** to Marah but were unable to drink the water. They then moved on to Elim where there were *seventy palm trees* (three-score and ten in KJV) and *twelve springs (wells).*

Three Days (3) times seventy palm trees (70) times twelve springs (12)

Equals

2,520

(3 * 70 * 12) is 2,520.

This story is recounted in Numbers 33, where the 42 stations of the Exodus are described. Notably, the Hebrew verb 'to camp' appears 42 times in this chapter. The number 42 is one-sixtieth of 2,520. In the base-60 numbering system, which we will cover in the next chapter, 2,520 is written $42,0_{base60}$.

The Number 2,520 Embedded in Daniel 3:1

Nebuchadnezzar the king made an image of gold, whose height was threescore cubits, and the breadth thereof six cubits: he set it up in the plain of Dura, in the province of Babylon. Daniel 3:1 KJV

In the first verse of Daniel 3, the dimensions of the golden image are the explicitly stated numbers of 60 cubits and 6 cubits.[6] 60*6=360. Additionally, "Image of gold," or "golden image," occurs seven times in the text of Daniel 3.

Image of Gold (7) times sixty cubits (60) times six cubits (6)

equals

2,520.

7*60*6=2,520

'Nebuchadnezzar' occurs 15 times in Daniel 3. 'King' occurs 21 times. The compound proper noun—'Nebuchadnezzar the king' or 'King Nebuchadnezzar'—occurs a total of eight times.[7]

Nebuchadnezzar' (15) times 'King' (21) times 'King Nebuchadnezzar' (8)

equals

2,520

15*21*8=2,520

The rest of this page is intentionally blank

---

[6] As a general rule of thumb, single digit numbers should be spelled out. With these equations it just makes more sense to write the numbers as digits rather than switching back and forth. Where the numbers are not equations I try to adhere to accepted practice.

[7] Daniel 3:1,2,3,5,7,9 and 24. Daniel 3:2 Nebuchadnezzar the king appears twice.

Daniel 6: Darius the Mede Creates a Government

It pleased Darius to set over the kingdom an hundred and twenty princes, which should be over the whole kingdom; And over these three presidents; of whom Daniel was first: that the princes might give accounts unto them, and the king should have no damage. Daniel 6:1-2

Daniel was placed at the head of the 120 princes. 'Daniel' occurs 21 times in the chapter.

120 'princes' (120) times 'Daniel' (21)

equals 2,520.

120*21=2,520.

Methods of Calculation

Okay, so let's regroup and assess what we have seen so far. I made a bold claim: numbers are embedded in some texts of the Bible that, when combined, create the common product of 2,520. We just looked at a couple of instances where this appears to be true. The basic rules work like this:

1. **If a cardinal number modifies a noun, the noun is assigned that discrete value.** *(Example: Daniel 3:1—60 cubits and 6 cubits; the nouns are assigned the value of the modifying number.)*
2. **Cardinal numbers in a narrative may be multiplied or added together** *(Example: Exodus 15—3 days, 70 palms, 12 springs).*
3. **Nouns without modifying numbers are assigned values based on their frequency of occurrence in the text** *(Example: Daniel 3:1—"king" (21), "Nebuchadnezzar" (15)).*
4. **Compound nouns may be assigned discrete values based on their frequency of occurrence in the text** *(Example Daniel 3:1—"Nebuchadnezzar the king" (8).*

This method of hiding a key, a message, or a code inside an existing message is known in code-making and codebreaking circles as steganography. Steganography is defined as, **"the branch of cryptography in which messages are hidden inside other**

messages."[8] Basically, a legitimate open message—in this case, a bit of scripture—contains a hidden message or key that would not normally be noticed by readers because it is obscured by the more obvious message.

When I first noticed these number patterns, it was a bit of a surprise. I originally thought that I might be imagining things. However, after continued investigation, I was forced to conclude that this is occurring in the Old Testament.

Some Old Testament writers, for reasons known only to them, embedded these numbers into the text of scripture. I was able to accept this thought pretty quickly. The writers of the Old Testament lived a long time ago; they had their own ways of doing things.

The obvious advantage of embedding equations in a text is that it protects the text from being miscopied. Since everything that was written had to be hand-copied by scribes, there had to be a way to protect the text from human error. The existence of the intact equations means that the text was faithfully transmitted to us, no matter how many times it was copied by hand. That was easy for me to accept. That's not what blew my mind.

What blew my mind is that it appears these numbers have prophetic implications when used in prophecy. These numbers, when observed as timelines, connect dates in the prophetic texts to dates of historical importance to the Jewish people or to Israel. No kidding.

I recognize that any person with a general level of skepticism will find my claims to be unbelievable. Somewhere, in the back of your mind, blaring like an unwelcome alarm on a Saturday morning, may be the thought: "Oh yeah, this guy stockpiles weapons, ammo, and food."

No Predictions!

So, let me put your mind at ease. There are no predictions in this book—none. I am not going to gather all my followers together in flowing white robes to receive the mothership. I am not going to

---

[8] "Steganography | Definition of Steganography by Webster's Online Dictionary." 2025. Webster-Dictionary.org. Accessed April 11, 2025. https://www.webster-dictionary.org/definition/Steganography.

predict the arrival of the Messiah, declare myself to be a modern-day Isaiah, or try to sell you a new brand of deodorant.

Conclusion

What you will find in this book are specific prophecies with their embedded equations well laid out. You can do the calculations yourself. You don't need to read Hebrew. I will show how those equations connect each specific prophecy to the Declaration of Establishment of the State of Israel.

First, however, we need to talk a little about ancient calendars and ancient math systems. The men who wrote these prophecies lived a long time ago—thousands of years ago. They experienced and understood the world differently. They had different calendars, different dating systems, and different ways of doing math. They saw the world differently. To understand these equations, we have to see things through older eyes—through their eyes.

There is no other way through this. The next couple of chapters are a bit dry. Hang in there, take notes, go slow. Most people are going to learn some new stuff in these next chapters.

Chapter Two

Ancient Math Systems, Base-60 and the Babylonians

Different Numbering Systems

Okay, so the first time that you find out that there is another way of expressing numbers besides the base-10 or decimal system, it can be a bit of a mind-blow. I was about 11 years old when I came across a book on mathematics in the library at Garden Home Elementary School. The book was titled something like, "The Magic of Numbers," or some other title to catch a child's eye. It was written for children, with pictures to spark the imagination, and charts to boil down hard topics.

Tucked away in the final chapters of that book, there was a discussion of other math systems, binary, octal, hexadecimal, and the Mayan numbers. The concepts were completely foreign to me. My eyes were opened to the fact that just as people can use different languages to express the same thought, they can also use different number systems to represent the same mathematical expression.

Just like "guten morgan," in German equals "good morning," in English, the decimal equation $1+1=2$ is expressed as $1+1=10$ in binary. Mind-blow.

People in the ancient world used different number systems. Not only did they use different symbols to represent numbers, but they also organized numbers differently. Our decimal system organizes numbers around multiples of ten. The Babylonians organized their numbers around multiples of 60.

Understanding Babylonian math is the key to understanding the embedded equations in scripture. Daniel lived in Babylon when he wrote his prophecies. He was educated in Babylon and wrote half of his book in the language of the Babylonian empire. The Assyrian and Babylonian empires were dominant in the world before and during the lifetimes of Jeremiah and Daniel. The Assyrians also used base-60 numbers. As hard as it may be to believe, it appears that Jeremiah also embedded equations in his prophecies using a base-60 system.

Ancient Babylonians used a different way of expressing numbers than what we use. This affected the way that they understood the world. We missed some of the number patterns in Daniel because we have been indoctrinated to understand the world using decimal numbers.

Base-60 and Babylonian Numbers[9]

Ancient Babylon's number system was based around the number 60. There are two ways of saying this. We could call this the sexagesimal system or we could refer to it as the base-60 system. For the sake of simplicity, I use the term base-60 instead of sexagesimal.

In the West, we use a base 10 number system or, more commonly, decimal number system. We have nine symbols that represent the natural numbers 1 through 9, and we have a symbol to represent the absence of value—0. We organize those symbols in columns from right to left. Each column advances by a factor of 10. So, we have a units column, a 10s column, a 100s column etc., each column increasing in value by a multiple of 10.

By comparison, the Babylonians system expressed natural numbers 1 through 59 using wedge-shaped symbols. They had no symbol to represent the absence of value. They had no zero. They organized their numbers in columns from right to left by factors of 60. So, they had a units column, a 60s column, 3600s, 216000s, etc., multiplying each successive column by 60.

The Babylonian Number System—no zero, no placeholder.

Our number system uses a zero to represent the absence of value. So, in the number 2,520, the zero in the units column represents the absence of value in that column. In this way, the number zero becomes a sort of placeholder. We know that the next number to the left, 2, represents value two in the 'tens' column or 20, because there is a zero as a placeholder in the units column. The 5 represents five 100s or 500, and the final 2 represents 2,000.

There is very little ambiguity in our system. This lack of ambiguity in our number system provides a great deal of stability.

---

[9] Babylonian numbers were adopted from "Babylonian Numerals Converter - Online Number System Calculator." n.d. www.dcode.fr. https://www.dcode.fr/babylonian-numbers.

When we write a number like 126, it basically can only be understood in one way.

The ancient Babylonians had no method to express the absence of value. They had no zero. They also had no placeholder to specify which column a number was in. They relied heavily on context to indicate whether a written number expressed values in the unit's column, 60s, or 3600s column.

The Babylonians wrote their numbers as a series of wedges. This is known formally as cuneiform writing, which just means "wedge shaped" writing. Vertically oriented wedges (up and down wedges) represented units; horizontally oriented wedges represented 10s.

These wedges were organized to represent the values 1 through 59. After that, the numbers started over in the next column. So, a single vertical wedge might represent the number one, or 60 or 3600 depending on which column it was in. Take a look at the chart below to see the numbers 1 through 59.

𒁹	1	𒌋𒁹	11	𒌋𒌋𒁹	21	𒌍𒁹	31	𒃻𒁹	41	𒐏𒁹	51
𒈫	2	𒌋𒈫	12	𒌋𒌋𒈫	22	𒌍𒈫	32	𒃻𒈫	42	𒐏𒈫	52
𒐈	3	𒌋𒐈	13	𒌋𒌋𒐈	23	𒌍𒐈	33	𒃻𒐈	43	𒐏𒐈	53
𒐉	4	𒌋𒐉	14	𒌋𒌋𒐉	24	𒌍𒐉	34	𒃻𒐉	44	𒐏𒐉	54
𒐊	5	𒌋𒐊	15	𒌋𒌋𒐊	25	𒌍𒐊	35	𒃻𒐊	45	𒐏𒐊	55
𒐋	6	𒌋𒐋	16	𒌋𒌋𒐋	26	𒌍𒐋	36	𒃻𒐋	46	𒐏𒐋	56
𒐌	7	𒌋𒐌	17	𒌋𒌋𒐌	27	𒌍𒐌	37	𒃻𒐌	47	𒐏𒐌	57
𒐍	8	𒌋𒐍	18	𒌋𒌋𒐍	28	𒌍𒐍	38	𒃻𒐍	48	𒐏𒐍	58
𒐎	9	𒌋𒐎	19	𒌋𒌋𒐎	29	𒌍𒐎	39	𒃻𒐎	49	𒐏𒐎	59
𒌋	10	𒌋𒌋	20	𒌍	30	𒃻	40	𒐏	50		

[10]

Looking at the chart above, then, we can see that the number 42 is represented by four horizontal wedges and two vertical wedges like this 𒃻𒈫 . However, that only represents 42 if the number is in the units column. If that symbol is in the 60s column, then it represents

[10] Space Awareness. "Counting and Reading the Hour in Cuneiform Digits." Accessed April 11, 2025. https://www.space-awareness.org/bg/activities/6053/counting-and-reading-the-hour-in-cuneiform-digits/.

42*60 or 2,520. If the symbol ⟪𝌆 is in the 3600s column, then it means 151,200 or 42*3600.

I know this is a bit complicated. The simplest way to think of this is, "multiply times 60, or 60 times 60." So, 42 times 60 equals 2,520; multiplied times 60 again it is 151,200. That's all that happened.

How Do We Express Base-60 Using Decimal Numbers

So, how can we, Westerners, create a base-60 expression using only ten discrete symbols? We will use the numbers 1 through 59 along with commas and 0s to express the fact that we are advancing by factors of 60. A subscript (little letters to the lower right) will identify the expression as base-60. So, the number $2,520_{base10}$ is expressed as $42,0_{base60}$. That is 42 in the 60s column and 0 in the units column (just think 42 * 60). The number 151,200 is $42,0,0_{base60}$ or 42 in the 3600s column (42 * 60 * 60).

The Babylonians during Daniel's lifetime did not have a zero or placeholder, so ⟪𝌆 could have represented 42, 2,520, or 151,200. So, 42_{base60}, $42,0_{base60}$, and $42,0,0_{base60}$ were all represented by four horizontal wedges and two vertical wedges ⟪𝌆. With no zero and no placeholder, the Babylonians had to rely on context to sort out whether the number represented units, 60s or some larger factor of 60.

By the 3rd century BC, the Babylonians developed a placeholder to indicate whether a number was in the units, 60s, or 3600s column. That symbol was two wedges canted at an angle. However, in Daniel's lifetime, this symbol was not in use.[11]

Observe the examples in the chart below to see how different values could be expressed in 6th century BC Babylon and third century BC Babylon. The canted wedges behave like zeros in our system.

---

[11] "Babylonian Cuneiform Numerals." Wikipedia. Last Modified April 2, 2025. Accessed April 10, 2025. https://en.wikipedia.org/wiki/Babylonian_cuneiform_numerals.

Decimal Value	Base-60	6th Century BC Babylonian	3rd Century BC Babylonian
42	42_{base60}		𒌋𒌋𒁹𒁹
2,520	$42,0_{base60}$	𒌋𒌋𒁹𒁹	𒌋𒌋𒁹𒁹𒌋
151,200	$42,0,0_{base60}$		𒌋𒌋𒁹𒁹𒌋𒌋
252	$4,12_{base60}$		𒐉𒌋𒁹𒁹
15,120	$4,12,0_{base60}$	𒐉𒌋𒁹𒁹	𒐉𒌋𒁹𒁹𒌋
907,200	$4,12,0,0_{base60}$		𒐉𒌋𒁹𒁹𒌋𒌋

Observe this next chart that organizes the numbers a little differently.

	Units	60s	3600s
Babylonian Number	𒌋𒌋𒁹𒁹	𒌋𒌋𒁹𒁹	𒌋𒌋𒁹𒁹
Base-60	42	$42,0_{base60}$	$42,0,0_{base60}$
Decimal Value	42	2,520	151,200
Babylonian Number	𒐉𒌋𒁹𒁹	𒐉𒌋𒁹𒁹	𒐉𒌋𒁹𒁹
Base-60	$4,12_{base60}$	$4,12,0_{base60}$	$4,12,0,0_{base60}$
Decimal Value	252	15,120	907,200

Conclusion

The Old Testament prophecies that we will be looking at were written by people who lived 2,500 years ago. They approached the world a little differently than we might. They had different methods for expressing numbers. They had different methods of expressing time and dates. As I said before, part of the reason we missed these number patterns is because we look at the world through Western eyes.

Chapter Three

Ancient Calendars, 'Prophetic' Calendars. Just How Long is a Year Anyway?

Defining our Terms; How Long is a Year?

Ask the proverbial 'man-on-the-street' how long a year is, and you will likely get the answer, '365 days, except on a leap year when we have 366 days,' or he will say, 'about 365 and a quarter days.' This is based on the Julian calendar year, first developed by Julius Caesar in 45 BC. This concept of a year is a pretty accurate version of a year, but it is not precise.[12]

A solar year, the number of days it takes for the earth to revolve around the sun, is about 365.24219 days. The actual length of each year varies slightly, but the differences are vanishingly small. For the sake of this book, I use a rounded measure of 365.242 days for a year. So, if I write 'solar year,' I mean a year of 365.242 days.

Egypt

The ancient Egyptian calendar year was 365 days long. They divided the year into 12 months of 30 days each and then added five days to the end of each year. This 365-day year lost one day in accuracy every four years. At the end of 1460 years, they skipped forward one full year in their year count.[13] In other words, their leap year really was an entire year, which they observed only once every 1,460 years.

Babylon

Ancient Babylon used what is called a luni-solar calendar. They used the phases of the moon and the position of the sun to keep track of calendar years. In most years, the Babylonian calendar contained 12 months. Since a lunar month only has about 29.5 days in it, their calendar year was about 354 days. Obviously, this loses 11

[12] Ray, Michael. 2019. "Julian Calendar | History & Difference from Gregorian Calendar." *Encyclopedia Britannica*. Last modified December 2024. Accessed April 10, 2025. https://www.britannica.com/science/Julian-calendar.
[13] Britannica editors. 1998. "Egyptian Calendar, Dating System." *Encyclopedia Britannica*. Last modified June 8, 2017. Accessed April 10, 2025. https://www.britannica.com/science/Egyptian-calendar#ref1248450

or 12 days a year. About seven years out of every 19, they inserted another month into the calendar—an intercalary month. So, the ancient Babylonian calendar year contained either 12 or 13 months.

The complexity of this system required careful observation of the moon and careful record-keeping. The Babylonians meticulously recorded the beginning of each month.[14] They kept these records on clay tablets, many of which have survived to our times.

Every month, astronomers in Babylon would mark the beginning of each lunar cycle and send out announcements across the empire. Archaeologists have found thousands of these clay tablets recording the lunar cycles. These tablets also announced whenever an intercalary month was added to the year.[15]

Archaeologists have been able to read these tablets, and thanks to the scholarship of people like Richard Parker and Waldo Dubberstein in their book, *Babylonian Chronology 626 BC—AD 75,* we have a very accurate idea of when events took place in ancient Babylon and Judah.

After the Babylonian captivity, the Jewish people adopted the Babylonian calendar, even adopting some of the month names. The modern Jewish religious calendar maintains this system. Because of this, when we look at dates in the Bible, we can be relatively certain that our conversions to modern calendars are accurate.

According to Parker and Dubberstein, these conversions have a margin of error of only one or two days.[16] The movements of celestial bodies are fairly consistent. As a result, we have a good idea of when any particular lunar month would have begun 2,500 years ago. Using this information, along with translated Babylonian records, has given us the ability to mark dates in the Old Testament with a precision of one or two days out of almost a million days.[17]

---

[14] Parker, Richard A, and Waldo H Dubberstein. 2007. *Babylonian Chronology 626 B.C.- A.D. 75.* Eugene, Or.: Wipf & Stock. 1-3.
[15] Parker and Dubberstein. 2007. 2.
[16] Parker and Dubberstein 2007. 25.
[17] A margin of error of one or two days out of 907,200 is 99.99978% accurate.

Numbering of the Years; Regnal Years of Kings

Most of the ancient world, including the writers of the Bible, marked the years according to the reigns of kings. As inefficient as this may seem, it apparently worked for them. The first year of a king did not begin when the king ascended to the throne. In Babylon and the Northern Kingdom of Israel, the first year of the king began on the first day of the first spring month of the year after he ascended to the throne. The intervening period was called the accession period.[18]

For instance, Nebuchadnezzar learned of his father's death while he was on campaign with the army in August of 605 BC. Nebuchadnezzar left the army and traveled back to Babylon. After arriving in Babylon in early September 605 BC, he took the throne. However, his first year was not marked until the spring month of Nisanu, in 604 BC. So, the first year of Nebuchadnezzar began on April 2, 604 BC. The months between September 605 BC and April 604 BC were the accession period.[19]

The Bible refers to regnal years of both Judah and Israel, who used different calendars. The calendar of ancient Judah began in the fall month of Tishri (Babylonian Tashrittu). This was around September or October each year. The northern kingdom of Israel reckoned the regnal years of their kings beginning in the spring. This has led to some confusion for interpreters of the Bible. Fortunately, modern scholarship has won out and helped clarify things for us considerably.

How Do We Know Our Dates are Accurate? This Was a Long Time Ago, After All.

Thanks to the careful study and scholarship of Edwin R. Thiele and others, we have a much more accurate idea of the dates in the Old Testament. Thiele was an Old Testament scholar who reconstructed the chronology of the kings of Judah and Israel. His most important work, and the one I refer to consistently in my research, was *The Mysterious Numbers of the Hebrew Kings*, first published in 1951.

---

[18] Thiele, Edwin R. 2004. *The Mysterious Numbers of the Hebrew Kings*. Grand Rapids, Mi: Kregel. 43-44 and 181.
[19] Thiele. 2004. 181 and 183-185.

All of the ancient dates that I reference in this book ultimately rely on the works of Thiele, and Parker and Dubberstein. I often reference *The Zondervan Press NIV Commentary,* and *The NIV Study Bible.* The dates in those works also originated from Thiele, and Parker and Dubberstein.

When Daniel referred to Babylonian and Persian kings, he used their calendrical system. When he referenced the king of Judah, he used Judah's calendar. The ancient dates in this book, with one exception, are based on the ancient Babylonian regnal years that began in the spring month of Nisanu (March or April).[20] The one exception comes from Daniel 1:1 and references the third year of Jehoiakim, which began on September 19, 606 BC. Daniel used the calendar of Judah, which began in the fall for this date.

Hey, What About This "Prophetic" Year Thing?

Sometimes you will run across interpreters of Old Testament prophecy who refer to a modified year of 360 days. There are some real arguments about this one. The simple fact is that nowhere in the Bible will you find the words, 'when thou readest the prophets thou shalt use a year of 360 days. Verily, the year shall be 360 days, and no other year shalt thou use.' That instruction doesn't exist. Nevertheless, there is significant circumstantial evidence to support the notion that sometimes Daniel and other prophets used a 360-day year.

Daniel actually used both solar years and 360-day years. In other words, he used 360-day periods, but he didn't use them exclusively. The embedded equations in Daniel and Jeremiah that I write about in the chapters that follow sometimes actually result in the number 907,200. This is the number of days in 2,520 years of 360 days each. I don't think that Daniel ever called these 360-day periods 'years.' I think he referred to them as 'times.' I have adopted this custom as well.

There is more than one respected interpreter of the Bible that occasionally uses this modified year of 360 days when discussing different passages of prophecy. John Walvoord, in his book, *Every*

---

[20] The modern Jewish religious calendar month of Nisan is the same as the ancient Babylonian month Nisanu. As a result, we have a modern apples-to-apples comparison with the ancient calendar.

Prophecy of the Bible, said, "In interpretation, the Bible authorizes the use of the prophetic year of 360 days."[21][22] Arno Gaebelein uses 360-day years as well to calculate times in Daniel.[23] J. Barton Payne, who wrote *Encyclopedia of Biblical Prophecy*, acknowledged that some scholars use the 360-day year to calculate Daniel's prophecies, but he did not elaborate or offer his own opinion.[24]

I include all of this because sometimes, among interpreters of the Bible, the discussions about details like this can get pretty heated. At times, it gets a little nasty. The arguments start to sound a little bit like a 1970's Hong Kong film: 'Look you! Our kung fu is the best, see!' I don't want to devolve into that. I've had to accept that Daniel used both solar years and 360-day 'times.'

I had my opinions several years ago but had to change them when I came across embedded number patterns in Daniel. These number patterns really leave little doubt. Sometimes Daniel embeds equations that result in 907,200 or the Babylonian equivalents of 15,120 or 252. In Daniel 5, he embeds the numbers 2,520 and 2484 right next to each other.[25] There are 2,484 solar years in 907,200 days.[26] So, confronted with the numbers, I had to change my opinion.

In this book you will read places where I refer to 'times;' this is a period of 360 days. When I use the term 'year,' I am referencing a solar year of 365.242 days.

I don't know for certain why Daniel used this modified year. There is some evidence that the ancient Babylonians used a 360-day

---

[21] Walvoord, John F. 2011. *Every Prophecy of the Bible: Clear Explanations for Uncertain Times.* Colorado Springs, Co: David C. Cook. 246.

[22] Actually, the Bible is infuriatingly silent on the topic. We infer permission to do this.

[23] Gaebelein, Arno Clemens. 1911. *The Prophet Daniel. A Key to the Visions and Prophecies of the Book of Daniel.* Second Edition. London; New York Printed: Marshall Bros. Kindle. Chapter 9.

[24] Payne, J Barton. 1973. *Encyclopedia of Biblical Prophecy: The Complete Guide to Scriptural Predictions and Their Fulfillment.* New York: Harper & Row. 386.

[25] See Appendix III in this book for details on Daniel 5. The arrangement of the nouns according to their frequency value really leaves little doubt.

[26] Rounding up.

year as a sort of 'shorthand' for certain astronomical calculations.[27][28] This may be why Daniel referred to a 'time' in some of his writings.

Time and Metaphors

Sometimes in the Bible, particularly in prophecy, a small thing can represent or foreshadow something big. Sometimes a day can represent a year and vice versa. Sometimes these metaphors manifest themselves literally in a prophetic way.

On occasion in prophetic texts, a day may represent a year. So, a passage that refers to 1,260 days might be understood to mean 1,260 years. This is not an unusual way of interpreting scripture, but it is not without controversy.

If you already believe that, prophetically, a day can represent a year, skip the rest of this chapter. You probably already know the arguments. If you are in a hurry and are willing to accept the premise that, on occasion, a day may represent a year, skip the rest of this chapter.

If you are unconvinced, or you've never heard of such a concept, please read on. If you just want to read the argument to understand where I am coming from, keep reading.

What is a Metaphor?

A metaphor is a symbolic method of using one thing to describe or understand another. Usually, metaphors attempt to describe something abstract or unfamiliar in terms of something more familiar or concrete.[29] The Bible uses many metaphors, including analogies, similes, parables, and poetic and symbolic language. Time itself is often described in metaphorical terms.

---

[27] Brack-Bernsen, Lis. n.d. "The 360-Day Year in Mesopotamia." Accessed March 25, 2025. https://epub.uni-regensburg.de/58013/1/31.the%20360%20day%20year.pdf.
[28] Horowitz, Wayne. 1996. "The 360- and 364-Day Year in Ancient Mesopotamia." *Journal of the Ancient Near Eastern Society 24 (1)*
[29] Underwood, Alice E.M. "What Is a Metaphor? —Definition and Examples | Grammarly." Last modified February 18, 2025. Accessed April 9, 2025. https://www.grammarly.com/blog/literary-devices/metaphor/?msockid=3990126e2b83659a095207d62a946454.

In the Bible, days and years are often equated. This is meant figuratively, but I think that sometimes the metaphor manifests itself literally in a prophetic sense. For instance, a week of days parallels a week of years in Leviticus 25. Each has its own Sabbath. The Sabbath year in Leviticus 25:1–12 parallels the Sabbath day. The 49 days between Passover and Shavuot have a parallel in the 49 years preceding the Jubilee.

A Day for a Year

The use of the word 'day' to represent years and 'years' to represent days, either prophetically, or for judgment, occurs in various places in scripture. In fact, the word 'day' is used in a variety of contexts in the Bible to describe various periods of time.

When is a Day not a Twenty-Four-Hour Period?

Days and years are closely associated in the opening chapters of Genesis. Genesis 2 uses the word 'day' to denote the week of creation: "These are the generations of the heavens and of the earth when they were created, **in the day** that the Lord God made the earth and the heavens," (Gen. 2:4 KJV). In Genesis 2:17, the LORD God warned Adam, "…for **in the day** that thou eatest thereof thou shalt surely die," (2:17 KJV). Adam died at 930 years old (Gen. 5:5). Since, "with the Lord a **day** is like a thousand years, and a thousand **years** are like a day," (2 Pet. 3:8) Adam literally died in the same 'day' that he ate the fruit.

Genesis 5 repeats the following pattern several times to describe the ages of the pre-flood patriarchs, "So, all the **days** of Seth were nine-hundred twelve **years**," (5:8). This pattern is used several times, 'So all the **days** of *(Some guy)* were *(really big number)* **years**.' In Genesis 6, God declared that the judgment of humanity was about to come when He says, "their **days** will be a hundred and twenty **years**."[30]

Moses was a shepherd in the wilderness of Midian for 40 years before he returned to his people in Egypt. Later on, he went up on Mount Sinai for 40 days before he returned to the people with the tablets of the law. So, Moses' two periods of separation from his people were mirrored by the number 40.

---

[30] Genesis 6:3

In Numbers 14:33–34, the Children of Israel were punished to wander in the wilderness for 40 years because the spies came back with a bad report and the people started complaining. The spies were gone for 40 days; the people were punished for 40 years. Again, 40 days and 40 years sort of mirrored one another.

Ezekiel's prophecies in Ezekiel 4 specifically assign a day for each year of Israel's sin and Judah's sin: "I have assigned you the same number of **days** as the **years** of their sin. So, for 390 days you will bear the sin of the people of Israel…and bear the sin of the people of Judah. I have assigned you 40 days, a **day** for each **year**."[31]

In Ezekiel 20, while in exile, exactly 49 days before Rosh Hashana, the elders came to Ezekiel hoping for a prophecy of good news. The LORD rebuked them, declaring that the past sins of their fathers would be punished. However, He promised to eventually bring them back and restore them to the land. That did happen, but it was 49 years after the temple was destroyed in 586 BC. So, the 49 days remaining before Rosh Hashana in Ezekiel 20 were mirrored by the 49 years between 586 BC and 537 BC.

The bottom line is this: metaphors are used throughout scripture. This is particularly true in prophetic texts. Sometimes those metaphors manifest themselves literally. A day representing a year or vice versa is used metaphorically in scripture. Sometimes that metaphor manifests itself literally in prophetic fulfillment.

---

[31] Ezekiel 4:5-6

Chapter Four

A Quick Introduction to the Five Main Chapters

Five Timelines: What to Expect Next

We've laid a lot of groundwork for these next five chapters. I originally wrote these next chapters as essays and eventually submitted them for copyright. As I continued my research, I realized they could form the core of a short book. So, I modified them slightly to function as chapters for this book. Each chapter focuses on a specific section of Israel's Declaration of Establishment.

The Events

The five modern events referenced in the Declaration are:

1. The birth of modern Zionism in the late 1890s.
2. The Balfour Declaration and the birth of Mandatory Palestine.
3. The Holocaust and WWII.
4. UN Resolution 181.
5. The Declaration of Establishment of the State of Israel.

Each of these five events is linked to the sixth century BC prophets Daniel and Jeremiah by timelines of 2,520 years or 2,520 'times' of 360 days.

Identify the Event and the End Date for the Timeline

Each of these next five chapters is constructed alike. First, I quote specific paragraphs out of the Declaration. I then provide a historical background for what is discussed in the Declaration, and I provide a date, if one has not already been identified.

Identify the Prophecy and the Start Date for the Timeline

Afterward, I identify a passage from either Daniel or Jeremiah that connects to the Declaration by an embedded timeline. I give background information for each scriptural passage, then I provide an analysis of the numbers. Finally, I point out parallels between the Old Testament prophecies and modern events.

If you would like to verify my work on the timelines, I recommend using the online tools available at "Julian Day and Date

Calculator," http://www.csgnetwork.com/juliandaydate.html. There are other tools available online, but this is the site that I used most often for my research.

The appendices at the back of this book include the full text of the Declaration of Establishment and the Balfour Declaration. Additionally, Appendix III provides a detailed analysis of noun frequencies in Daniel 5.

Let's dive in.

Chapter Five

Theodor Herzl and Jeremiah 32

In the year 5657 (1897), at the summons of the spiritual father of the Jewish State, Theodor Herzl, the First Zionist Congress convened and proclaimed the right of the Jewish people to national rebirth in its own country.[32]

The third paragraph of modern Israel's Declaration of Establishment recalls the birth of modern Zionism, naming Theodor Herzl as the spiritual father of the Jewish state. While previous paragraphs in the Declaration mention historical events, this is the first paragraph that names a specifically dated event or person.

Theodor Herzl

Theodor Herzl, a man perhaps not well known today outside of Jewish circles and Israeli textbooks, was a historic and pivotal personality. Though he lived only 44 years, he laid the foundation for the modern Zionist movement.

Herzl was born in Hungary, educated in Austria, and eventually moved to France in the 1890s, where he worked as a journalist. Alarmed by the growing antisemitism that he saw in Western Europe, Herzl became convinced that there was no solution to modern antisemitism apart from the creation of a Jewish homeland in what is now known as modern Israel.[33][34]

In the 1890s, Herzl began working to organize influential Jews in Western Europe, eventually arranging the first Zionist Congress in

[32]"The Declaration of the Establishment of the State of Israel." Israel Ministry of Foreign Affairs Website. 2024. www.gov.il. Accessed March 18, 2025. https://www.gov.il/en/pages/declaration-of-establishment-state-of-israel.

[33] Ben-Gurion, David. 2019. "Theodor Herzl | Austrian Zionist Leader." *Encyclopedia Britannica*. Last modified March 2, 2025. Accessed April 10, 2025. https://www.britannica.com/biography/Theodor-Herzl.

[34] Jewish Virtual Library. 2015. "Theodor (Binyamin Ze'ev) Herzl." Accessed April 10, 2025. https://www.jewishvirtuallibrary.org/theodor-binyamin-ze-rsquo-ev-herzl.

Basel, Switzerland in 1897.[35] The Zionist Congress agreed that their specific goal was to create a Jewish homeland in Palestine. Herzl understood the importance of what was accomplished in Basel, writing in his diary words that would prove to be prescient.

> *Were I to sum up the Basel Congress in a word—which I shall be very careful not to do publicly—it would be this: At Basel I founded the Jewish state. If I said this out loud today, I would be answered by universal laughter. Perhaps in five years, and certainly fifty, everyone will admit it.[36]*

Herzl's opening speech in Basel, delivered on the first day of the Congress, August 29, 1897, left no doubt that he believed there should be a Jewish homeland in Palestine.[37] A little more than one year after the First Zionist Congress, Herzl negotiated for the creation of a Jewish homeland with Kaiser Wilhelm II during the Kaiser's visit to Jerusalem.[38]

Herzl's meeting with Wilhelm II was his most important diplomatic accomplishment. Wilhelm II had heard about the First Zionist Congress and was interested in meeting Herzl. After some initial diplomatic overtures, Herzl first received word that the Kaiser was interested in hearing from him about the Zionist cause in early October 1898.[39]

Answering an invitation from the Kaiser, Herzl eventually traveled to the Levant, his ship arriving in Jaffa on October 26. He met with the Kaiser in Jerusalem on November 2, 1898. Unfortunately, the meeting was a disappointment, because the Kaiser did not take the creation of a Jewish state seriously.[40]

Nevertheless, it was an important step forward toward the birth of Israel. This was the first time that a modern nation publicly

[35] Jewish Virtual Library. 2015. "Theodor (Binyamin Ze'ev) Herzl." Accessed April 10, 2025. https://www.jewishvirtuallibrary.org/theodor-binyamin-ze-rsquo-ev-herzl.

[36] Avineri, Shlomo. 2013. *Herzl*. Hachette UK. 141.

[37] Avineri, Shlomo. 2013. 156-157.

[38] Jewish Virtual Library. 2015. "Theodor (Binyamin Ze'ev) Herzl." Accessed April 10, 2025. https://www.jewishvirtuallibrary.org/theodor-binyamin-ze-rsquo-ev-herzl.

[39] Avineri, Shlomo. 2013. 5.

[40] Avineri, Shlomo. 2013. 14, 20-21.

entertained the idea of creating a Jewish homeland in the middle east.[41]

Though this attempt was not successful, Herzl continued to meet with other international leaders over the next few years, including maintaining conversations with the Ottoman Sultan.[42]

It was both his actions in Basel, Switzerland, and his negotiations with the Kaiser and the Sultan that caused him to be seen as the spiritual father of Israel. The Jewish people recognized him as their representative in achieving the dream of a Jewish homeland. The international community also recognized him as the representative of the Zionist movement.

Prophetically speaking, Herzl fulfilled the ancient role of kinsman redeemer for all the Jewish people when he met with Wilhelm II in 1898. Herzl stepped forward and negotiated for the return of the land to his fellow Jews. As part of his proposal, he suggested paying off the Ottoman Empire's foreign debt in return for allowing the migration of Jews to Palestine.[43] Theodor Herzl attempted to do for his people what the prophet Jeremiah had done for his cousin 25 centuries earlier.[44]

Forty-nine years later, on November 29, 1947, the United Nations adopted Resolution 181, creating the modern state of Israel in what had been Mandatory Palestine.[45] Fifty years after his meeting with the Kaiser, Israel declared her independence. Herzl's meeting with the Kaiser in 1898 forms the endpoint for our timeline.

---

[41] Avineri, Shlomo. 2013. *Herzl.* Hachette UK. 4, 14 and 21-26.

[42] Avineri, Shlomo. 2013. *Herzl.* Hachette UK. 200-202.

[43] Gjevori, Elis. "How Theodor Herzl Failed to Convince the Ottomans to Sell Palestine." n.d. Accessed April 9, 2025. *TRTWorld.*
https://www.trtworld.com/magazine/how-theodor-herzl-failed-to-convince-the-ottomans-to-sell-palestine-46991.

[44] Jeremiah 32

[45] United Nations. 1947. "Palestine Plan of Partition with Economic Union - General Assembly Resolution 181." Question of Palestine. November 29, 1947. Accessed April 11, 2025. https://www.un.org/unispal/document/auto-insert-185393/.

Jeremiah 32 and Theodor Herzl, an Interesting Connection

Jeremiah 32 recounts events that took place in April 587 BC. The prophet Jeremiah, acting as a kinsman redeemer, purchased a plot of land from his cousin. After providing some background, I will show how this episode connects prophetically to Theodor Herzl and the Independence of modern Israel.

Kinsman Redeemer

The story in Jeremiah 32 highlights the custom of the kinsman redeemer in Jewish law. Almost half the verses in the chapter detail the purchase of the land and Jeremiah's prayer to God basically asking, "why did I just buy this land, LORD?"[46]

In ancient Israel, when people needed money—whether because of bad luck or bad judgment—they could sell their land.[47] Normally, the land was sold within the extended family. A cousin, an uncle, or some other relative was given the chance to buy the land first. This custom prevented a family from losing their inheritance permanently.[48][49]

The land could not be sold forever. The land had to be returned to the original owner eventually. If the original owners could not afford to buy the land back, it would revert to their ownership when the Jubilee year arrived.[50] On Rosh Hashanah, in the Jubilee year, all slaves were freed, all debts cleared, and land deeds reverted to the original owners. What God had granted could be sold or lost temporarily, but never permanently lost.

In Jeremiah 32, the prophet recounted an episode in his own life which had prophetic implications for the nation. The overarching theme of the story is redemption. Jeremiah acted as kinsman redeemer for his cousin who apparently needed money. The cousin

---

[46] Jeremiah 32:25 my paraphrase.
[47] Jewish Encyclopedia. n.d. "GO'EL." Accessed April 11, 2025. https://www.jewishencyclopedia.com/articles/6734-go-el.
[48] Leviticus 25:13-17 and 25-28
[49] Guzik, David. 2022. "Study Guide for Jeremiah 32." Blue Letter Bible.org. June 16, 2022. Accessed April 10, 2025. https://www.blueletterBible.org/comm/guzik_david/study-guide/jeremiah/jeremiah-32.cfm.
[50] Leviticus 25:25-28

visited Jeremiah in prison, asking Jeremiah to buy his land as a near kinsman. There is a bit of irony in this story, as Jeremiah was in prison—the cousin should have been helping Jeremiah, not the other way around.

God told Jeremiah to buy his cousin's land for 17 shekels of silver—a number rich in symbolism. In Hebrew numerology, the name of God, YHVH, holds the value 26 or 17.[51]

Jeremiah obeyed the LORD's command and then he announced to the witnesses present, "For thus saith the LORD of hosts, the God of Israel; houses and fields and vineyards shall be possessed again in this land."[52]

At first blush, it appears that Jeremiah understood exactly what he was doing, but he made this statement despite harboring serious doubts. Once he settled the business with his cousin, he immediately prayed to God asking, "why did You have me purchase the land, when we are overrun with enemies and about to be destroyed?"[53]

God answered Jeremiah by predicting that people would one day return to the land, and when they did, buying and selling land would be a normal occurrence. This prophecy had two fulfillments, one in the 6th century BC and one in the modern age. Jeremiah 32:44 contains the promise of that return.

> Men shall buy fields for money, and subscribe evidences, and seal them, and take witnesses in the land of Benjamin, and in the places about Jerusalem, and in the cities of Judah, and in the cities of the mountains, and in the cities of the valley, and in the cities of the south: for I will cause their captivity to return, saith the LORD. Jeremiah 32:44

This prophecy is dated April 23, 587 BC, marking the beginning of our timeline.[54][55] At that moment, Jerusalem was under siege and

---

[51] There is more than one method of Hebrew numerology. The most common and well known calculates a value 26. The second most common method calculates a value of 17 for YHVH.

[52] Jeremiah 32:15

[53] Jeremiah 32:23-25 my paraphrase

[54] Parker, Richard A, and Waldo H Dubberstein. 2007. *Babylonian Chronology 626 B.C.- A.D. 75*. Eugene, Or.: Wipf & Stock. 28.

[55] Jeremiah 32:1

much of Judah was occupied by Babylonian troops. The situation appeared as hopeless as it could be. In fact, in less than a year-and-a-half, Jerusalem and the Temple were destroyed in 586 BC.[56]

Jeremiah's prophecy came to pass 49 years after the temple was destroyed. In 538 BC, the Persian King Cyrus gave orders that the Jewish exiles should return to Jerusalem to rebuild the city and the Temple.[57]

On Rosh Hashanah 537 BC,[58] the first returned exiles offered sacrifices on a rebuilt altar in Jerusalem.[59] This was exactly 49 years and 49 days after July 18 and 19, 586 BC, when Jerusalem's walls were breached and King Zedekiah captured.[60] Those exiles observed the various religious holy days of the seventh month in 537 BC, exactly 49 years after the destruction of Jerusalem.[61][62]

The prophetic connection linking this verse to Jewish exiles is not limited to the 6th century BC. There is a modern connection to the Diaspora as well. Embedded in the text of Jeremiah's prophecy are a series of numbers that form a timeline connected to modern Zionism, particularly to Theodor Herzl.

> *Men shall buy fields for money, and subscribe evidences, and*
> *seal them, and take witnesses in the land of Benjamin...*
> *Jeremiah 32:44*

If we look at the Hebrew nouns that make up this verse and analyze their frequency of occurrence, we can derive an equation. By assigning values to the nouns based on how often they appear in the

---

[56] Jeremian 52:12-15

[57] Ezra 1:1-4; Isaiah 44:28, 45:1-3

[58] Barker, Kenneth L, and Donald W Burdick. 1995. *The NIV Study Bible*. Grand Rapids, Mi: Zondervan Pub. House. 669 margin notes Ezra 3:1.

[59] Ezra 3:2-3

[60] Jeremiah 52:6-11 The city walls were breached on July 18th. King Zedekiah and some portion of his army escaped by night. He was captured, most likely the next day, and brought before Nebuchadnezzar.

[61] Parker, Richard A, and Waldo H Dubberstein. 2007. *Babylonian Chronology 626 B.C.- A.D. 75*. Eugene, Or.: Wipf & Stock. 28. 537 BC, Seventh month 9/6.

[62] Rosh Hashana was on September 6, 537 BC. This was 17,947 days after the king was capture on July 19, 586 BC. With 17,898 days in 49 solar years, this is 49 years and 49 days.

chapter we get the following values:[63] fields (7), money (or silver) (5), evidence (or deeds) (9), witness (4), and Land of Benjamin (2).

The chart below shows these nouns and their frequencies of occurrence in the chapter. The chart shows the English translation, the Hebrew word, the Strong's Concordance value, and its frequency of occurrence in Jeremiah 32.

Multiplied together, the value of these nouns equals 2,520. In this timeline, 2,520 'times' of 360 days each are used. Counting forward from the date of Jeremiah's prophecy, April 23, 587 BC, a timeline of 2,520 'times' (907,200 days), we arrive in February of 1898 AD.[64] Later that year, "in the burning noonday sun," on November 2, 1898, Theodor Herzl met with Kaiser Wilhelm II to discuss the creation of a Jewish homeland.[65][66]

Noun	Hebrew	Strong's	Occurrence
Fields	שׂדת	H7704	7
Money/silver	כסף	H3701	5
Evidence/deed	ספר	H5612	9
Witness	עד	H5707	4
Land of Benjamin	ארץ בנימן		2

A Repetition of Base-60 Values Links Jeremiah and Herzl

In an earlier chapter, I discussed the importance of base-60 numbers to understanding these prophetic timelines. The 907,200 days in our timeline are expressed in base-60 numbers as $4,12,0,0_{base60}$. There is an interesting equivalence to the number 252 in base-60, because **907,200** is **252 times 60 times 60**. In base-60, **252**

[63] Sefaria. 2023. "Jeremiah 32:44." Accessed April 11, 2025. https://www.sefaria.org/Jeremiah.32.44?lang=b. The original Hebrew does not include the word 'men.' The original seems to read more like, "fields shall be bought…"

[64] "Julian Day and Date Time Calculator." n.d. www.csgnetwork.com. Accessed April 11, 2025. http://www.csgnetwork.com/juliandaydate.html.
[65] Avineri, Shlomo. 2013. *Herzl*. Hachette UK. 20-21.
[66] Shlomo Avineri actually quotes Herzl's writings in declaring it was the noon day sun.

is written $4,12_{base60}$. In Babylon cuneiform numbers, both were written, 𒁹 𒌋 𒐖.

Adding **252** days to our timeline, or $4,12_{base60}$ **days**, we end up on October 23, 1898. This was within a few days of Herzl's arrival in Palestine to negotiate with Wilhelm II. Ten and a half days later, around noon, or **252 hours** later, Herzl met personally with Wilhelm II on November 2, 1898.

This creates an intriguing timeline pattern: the number of days from Jeremiah's prophecy to October 23, 1898, was **907,452** or in base-60, $4,12,4,12_{base60}$ **days**, followed by **252** hours, $4,12_{base60}$ hours.

Parallels Between Jeremiah in 587 BC and Herzl in 1898 AD

The parallels between Herzl and Jeremiah are striking. During the lifetimes of both men, Palestine was under Gentile occupation. Forty-nine years after Jeremiah acted as a kinsman redeemer, the Gentile king, Cyrus the Great, gave orders for the exiles to return to Jerusalem. Forty-nine years after Herzl negotiated with Wilhelm II, the United Nations adopted UN Resolution 181, calling for the creation of the state of Israel in Mandatory Palestine, November 29, 1947.

In antiquity, fifty years after Jeremiah bought his cousin's land, the exiles returned to Jerusalem and began rebuilding.[67] This foreshadowed the fifty years between Herzl's negotiation with Wilhelm II in 1898, and Israel's independence in 1948.

In the 6th century BC, fifty years after the events recorded in Jeremiah 32, the Babylonian Empire was conquered and divided by its enemies. In modern history, fifty years after the Ottoman Empire and Germany refused Herzl's negotiations, both nations were likewise conquered and divided by enemies.

In both cases, a great persecution of Jews took place before their return to Israel.[68] Neither Jeremiah nor Herzl lived to see their people return to their homeland.[69]

---

[67] Jeremiah bought the land in 587 BC. The exiles returned in 537 BC.
[68] Scholars differ on when Jeremiah died, but it was most likely in the 570s BC.
[69] Herzl died in 1904.

Israel's Declaration of Establishment names Herzl specifically as "the spiritual father of the Jewish state." His most politically important act—negotiating with Wilhelm II in Jerusalem—is linked to the Old Testament prophet, Jeremiah, by a timeline of 2,520 'times.' If this were the only prophetic connection associated with the 2,520, I would not dare write about it. However, there are at least four other prophetic connections in the Declaration, and the accuracy of a couple of these timelines is jaw-dropping.

Chapter Six

The Balfour Declaration

Historic Events of 1917 Referenced in the Declaration

This right was recognized in the Balfour Declaration of the 2nd of November, 1917, and reaffirmed in the Mandate of the League of Nations which, in particular, gave international sanction between the Jewish people and Eretz-Israel and to the right of the Jewish people to rebuild its national home.

The Declaration of the Establishment of the State of Israel, Fourth Paragraph[70]

The fourth paragraph of the Declaration of Establishment references the Balfour Declaration, signed on November 2, 1917. The importance of this document to modern Zionism cannot be overstated. Prior to modern Israel's independence in 1948, Jews living in Mandatory Palestine commemorated Balfour Day much like citizens of other nations celebrate their nation's birth.

The period from November through December of 1917 was important in the history of Jerusalem and modern Zionism, forming the endpoint of this chapter's timeline.[71] Within six weeks of the Balfour declaration, British troops occupied the city of Jerusalem, ending the Ottoman Sultan's control over Palestine. A new king had taken charge of Jerusalem's future.

November 1917, WWI, and the Balfour Letter

By November 1917, WWI had been raging in Europe and the Middle East for three years. In early November 1917, the Egyptian Expeditionary Forces, under the command of British General

---

[70] "The Declaration of the Establishment of the State of Israel." Israel Ministry of Foreign Affairs Website. 2024. www.gov.il. Accessed March 18, 2025. https://www.gov.il/en/pages/declaration-of-establishment-state-of-israel.
[71] Engelmayer, Jay. 2022. "The Balfour Declaration & the Mandate for Palestine - 1917 - 1922." *The Judean.* May 23, 2022. Accessed April 10, 2025. https://thejudean.com/index.php/history/64-the-balfour-declaration-the-mandate-for-palestine-1917-1922.

Edmund Allenby, were already advancing on the city of Jerusalem.[72] Allenby had defeated Ottoman forces at Beersheba in October of 1917. In early November, Allenby's army also broke the Ottoman defense at Gaza in what is now known as the 3rd Battle of Gaza. From that point on, the Ottoman army in Palestine was more or less continuously in retrograde.[73]

While the British army was on the advance in Palestine, British diplomacy moved forward as well. British Foreign Secretary, Arthur James Balfour, wrote a letter to Lord Rothschild, a prominent leader in the British Jewish community. Balfour's letter expressed the British government's support for the establishment of a Jewish homeland in Palestine. A short excerpt from that letter is below:

> *His Majesty's Government view with favour the establishment in Palestine of a national home for the Jewish people, and will use their best endeavors to facilitate the achievement of this object,*[74]

Dated November 2, 1917, the Balfour letter was published in newspapers a week later on November 9, 1917.[75] The letter had significant implications for the Middle East, particularly for what would happen after WWI. The British occupation of Palestine combined with the Balfour Declaration significantly changed the geopolitical landscape in the Levant. Not only had the British publicly stated their support for creating a Jewish homeland in Palestine, but they also had the practical power to make it happen.[76]

---

[72] "The Palestine Campaign: How Britain Captured Jerusalem in World War One." History Hit. December 6, 2018. Accessed April 11, 2025. https://www.historyhit.com/1917-general-allenby-enters-jerusalem/
[73] Jewish Virtual Library. n.d. "Turks Surrender Jerusalem to the British." Accessed April 11, 2025. https://www.jewishvirtuallibrary.org/general-edmond-allenby-marches-into-jerusalem.
[74] My Jewish Learning. 2009. "The Balfour Declaration Full Text." My Jewish Learning. Accessed April 10, 2025. https://www.myjewishlearning.com/article/read-the-balfour-declaration/.
[75] Britannica editors. 2025. "Balfour Declaration | History & Impact." *Encyclopedia Britannica.* Accessed April 10, 2025. https://www.britannica.com/event/Balfour-Declaration.
[76] Ettinger, Shmuel. n.d. "The Balfour Declaration of 1917." Reprinted by My Jewish Learning. Accessed April 11, 2025. https://www.myjewishlearning.com/article/the-balfour-declaration/.

By mid-November 1917, Allenby's forces approached the Judean hills outside Jerusalem. Though sources vary somewhat, the battle of Jerusalem began around mid-November 1917 and continued until Ottoman forces fully withdrew from the city on December 8. On December 11, 1917, Allenby marched into Jerusalem through the Jaffa gate.

After 400 years of Ottoman rule, the city of Jerusalem passed to the control of a new king, a British king. The first regnal year of the new king, according to Babylonian reckoning, began on March 14, 1918.[77] The conquest of Jerusalem by British forces and the reign of a new king over Jerusalem mark the modern endpoint of a timeline connected to the story in Daniel 2.

Daniel Chapter 2: 2,520 Years from 603 BC to AD 1918

Daniel 2 recounts a story set in the second year of Nebuchadnezzar, which began on March 22, 603 BC.[78] Sometime during that year, King Nebuchadnezzar was deeply disturbed by a dream. Obsessed with his kingdom and what would come after he was gone, the king had dreamed of an enormous statue that was brilliant and terrifying. He knew the dream was significant, but he could not interpret its meaning.

Daniel, one of the king's advisors, interpreted the dream for Nebuchadnezzar. The statue represented the various Gentile empires that would dominate the Middle East and the destiny of Jerusalem. The different sections of the statue represented Babylon and the empires that followed her. A final kingdom, the Kingdom of God—represented by a great stone—would destroy and replace all previous human kingdoms.

The image was composed of **seven** distinct body parts (head, arms and chest, belly and thighs, and legs and feet).[79] **Six** materials, (gold, silver, bronze, iron, clay, and stone) represented **five** kingdoms (four human kingdoms and the kingdom of God). **Four** precious

---

[77] The Jewish month Nisan (Babylonian Nisanu) began on March 14 in 1918. As I pointed out in chapter three, the Babylonians and Israel began their year in the spring.

[78] Parker, Richard A, and Waldo H Dubberstein. 2007. *Babylonian Chronology 626 B.C.- A.D. 75*. Eugene, Or.: Wipf & Stock. 27.

[79] 'Thighs' might also be translated 'sides' or 'loins.'

metals (gold, silver, bronze, and iron) represented the Gentile empires. Daniel gave **three** visual descriptions of the image, the image was enormous, brilliant, and terrifying. These numbers, the **seven** body parts, **six** materials, **five** kingdoms, **four** precious metals and **three** visual descriptions multiplied together, equal 2,520.

$$7*6*5*4*3 = 2,520$$

In my book, *2520: The Hidden Key in the Book of Daniel*, I demonstrated that the text of Daniel contains numerous embedded equations that either reveal the numbers 2,520, 907,200, or their base-60 equivalents. Remarkably, more than ten of these equations can be found in Daniel 2 alone. I will not detail all of them here.

Daniel 2 contains a division in the original languages. The first few verses of the chapter are in Hebrew; the rest of the chapter is written in Aramaic. This linguistic division of the chapter is connected to Daniel's formula for embedding equations in the text.

The key to understanding Daniel 2 is the word 'king.' The dream was given to the king. The dream was about the kings that would dominate the Middle East and Jerusalem. Daniel declared that God "sets up kings and deposes kings."[80]

The word "king" appears 48 times in Daniel 2—six occurrences in the first four Hebrew verses, and 42 occurrences in the remaining Aramaic verses (Daniel 2:5-49). When we multiply 6 by 42, the result is 252, which is one-tenth of 2,520—a number central to prophetic symbolism in this chapter.

The story in Daniel 2 took place in Nebuchadnezzar's second regnal year as king of Babylon, which began in the spring of 603 BC.[81] Measuring 2,520 solar years from the Babylonian Spring month of Nisanu in 603 BC, (March 22, 603 BC), brings us to the

---

[80] Daniel 2:21, my paraphrase.
[81] Parker, Richard A, and Waldo H Dubberstein. 2007. *Babylonian Chronology 626 B.C.- A.D. 75.* Eugene, Or.: Wipf & Stock. 27.

first day of the Jewish month of Nisan[82][83][84]—March 14, 1918. By Babylonian reckoning, this was the first regnal year that the king of Great Britain controlled Jerusalem.

This timeline creates a connection between Nebuchadnezzar, the first Gentile king in antiquity to control Judah and Jerusalem, and the last Gentile king in modern times to control both Judah and Jerusalem. Daniel embedded the 2,520-year timeline in his description of the statue. The statue symbolized not just the next few empires that followed Babylon, but the long march of Gentile empires which would control Jerusalem for 25 centuries.

A Long March of History

The emphasis of Daniel 2 is on the kingdoms that would shape and dominate the future of Jerusalem. All of history has been marching toward the moment when the Jewish people would regain control of their own land. The publication of the Balfour Declaration and the capture of Jerusalem by British forces in 1917 were critically important milestones in this march of history.

In this march of history, God connected the first Gentile kingdom to the last Gentile kingdom by a span of 2,520 years. Daniel embedded that number in the description of the statue.

Jeremiah 36 and the Battle of Jerusalem in 1917; A 2,520 Year Timeline

According to Jeremiah 36:9, the events in Jeremiah 36 took place on November 24, 604 BC,[85][86] during the reign of Jehoiakim. This was a little more than a year after Babylon first took Jewish captives into

[82] The Jewish people adopted names of months from the Babylonian calendar during the Babylonian captivity in the 6th century BC. Nisanu became Nisan, Tashrittu became Tishri, Adaru became Adar, etc. They continue to use those months in their religious calendar to this day.
[83] HebCal. n.d. "Jewish Calendar 1918 Diaspora - Hebcal." Hebcal.com. Accessed April 11, 2025.
https://www.hebcal.com/hebcal?year=1918&v=1&yt=G&nx=on&D=on&d=on&c=off&maj=on&min=on&mod=on&mf=on&ss=on.
[84] "Julian Day and Date Time Calculator." n.d. www.csgnetwork.com. http://www.csgnetwork.com/juliandaydate.html. March 14, 1918.
[85] Parker, Richard A, and Waldo H Dubberstein. 2007. *Babylonian Chronology 626 B.C.- A.D. 75.* Eugene, Or.: Wipf & Stock. 27. Ninth Month 11/24 604 BC
[86] Jeremiah 36:9, the ninth month, Chislev, began on November 24.

exile in the fall of 605 BC[87]—a group that included the prophet, Daniel.

In 604 BC, Jeremiah prophesied that the recent problems with Babylon were only the beginning. In Jeremiah 25, he predicted that Babylon would not only bring suffering to Judah, but to all her neighbors. Jeremiah instructed Baruch, his assistant, to write down these prophecies and read them to the people in the hope that this would lead them to repentance (Jer. 36:5-7).

The Jewish king, Jehoiakim, listened to Jeremiah's prophecies but, in defiance, deliberately destroyed the scroll. With a knife, he cut the scroll into sections and burned them one at a time. Jeremiah 36 emphasizes the significance of this act, explicitly stating five times that the king burned the scroll.

November 24, 604 BC—the date of Jeremiah's prophecy in Jeremiah 36—serves as the starting point of this timeline. Exactly 2,520 years later, in 1917, British forces captured Jerusalem. Observe the numbers below.

Jeremiah 36:29

> *And thou shalt say to Jehoiakim king of Judah, thus saith the LORD; Thou hast burned this roll, saying, Why hast thou written therein, saying, The king of Babylon shall certainly come and destroy this land, and shall cause to cease from thence man and beast? Jeremiah 36:29*

The embedded equation in this verse incorporates the verb 'to burn' (Strong's H8313),[88] which occurs five times in the chapter. This differs a bit from most of the equations in Jeremiah, which typically do not include verbs. However, in this verse, the prominence of 'burning the scroll' in the narrative seems to indicate that the verb should be used in the equation as well.

The frequency values of the words and phrases—Jehoiakim (6), 'King of Judah' (6), roll (14), and 'burned the roll' or 'burn' (5)—

---

[87] Thiele, Edwin R. 2004. *The Mysterious Numbers of the Hebrew Kings*. Grand Rapids, Mi: Kregel. 183.

[88] All Strong's Concordance Values are taken from BlueletterBible.org.

multiplied together equal 2,520. Observe the table below for a detailed account.

Noun	Hebrew	Strong's	Occurrence
Jehoiakim	יהויקים	H3079	6
King of Judah	מלך־יהודה	Compound Noun	6
Roll	המגלה	H5612	14
burned	שׂרף	H8313	5
King	מלך	H4428	19
Babylon	בבל	H894	1
Land	ארץ	H776	1
Man	אדם	H120	1
Beast	בהמה	H929	1

The reader may wish to take this calculation with a grain of salt. The word LORD is not incorporated into the calculation. It may be that Jeremiah departed from his normal methods of embedding numbers, or that the original order of the words was altered. It may also be that scribes—unaware of the embedded equations—added the word LORD an additional time in the chapter to achieve a numerically significant 17 occurrences of that word.

Counting 2,520 solar years (920,409 days) from November 24, 604 BC brings us to November 17, 1917. This date falls during the battle for Jerusalem in World War I.

The remaining nouns have a combined sum of 23. I don't know if this number should be considered in the timeline calculations, but I include it because a remarkable coincidence occurs when we add this number to the overall calculation.

Add 23 days (the sum of the remaining nouns) to November 17, and we arrive on December 10, 1917, which is the day before Allenby marched into Jerusalem. Turkish forces fled the city on December 8. British General Allenby entered the city on December 11.

Exactly 2,520 years after Jeremiah warned that the king of Babylon would seize control of Jerusalem, a modern king of Babylon lost control of the city. The Ottoman Empire had controlled the ruins of ancient Babylon for 400 years; therefore, the Sultan was technically the "king of Babylon."[89] In December of 1917, Jerusalem passed to the control of King Edward V of England. All of this occurred exactly 2,520 years after Jeremiah's prophecy.

The Balfour Declaration marked the first time that a modern nation publicly declared its support for the creation of a Jewish homeland in Palestine. By defeating the Ottoman armies in Palestine, the British Empire gained the ability to implement the Balfour Declaration. Incredibly, these events occurred 2,520 years after Jehoiakim burned the scroll and after Nebuchadnezzar's dream of the great statue.

At this point, we have two historic events in the Declaration of Establishment which align with Bible prophecy through timelines embedded in scripture. There are three more instances like this in the Declaration.

---

[89] Baghdad and the ruins of Babylon came under British control in 1917 as well.

Chapter Seven

The Holocaust and WWII

The catastrophe which recently befell the Jewish people - the massacre of millions of Jews in Europe - was another clear demonstration of the urgency of solving the problem of its homelessness by re-establishing in Eretz-Israel the Jewish State, which would open the gates of the homeland wide to every Jew and confer upon the Jewish people the status of a fully privileged member of the comity of nations.

Survivors of the Nazi holocaust in Europe, as well as Jews from other parts of the world, continued to migrate to Eretz-Israel, undaunted by difficulties, restrictions and dangers, and never ceased to assert their right to a life of dignity, freedom and honest toil in their national homeland.

In the Second World War, the Jewish community of this country contributed its full share to the struggle of the freedom- and peace-loving nations against the forces of Nazi wickedness and, by the blood of its soldiers and its war effort, gained the right to be reckoned among the peoples who founded the United Nations.

Declaration of the Establishment of the State of Israel, paragraphs five through seven.[90]

These three paragraphs of the Declaration reference the Holocaust and World War II. These dual tragedies—shaped by human suffering—are foreshadowed in certain prophecies found in Daniel and Jeremiah. Remarkably, each prophecy is linked to these catastrophes through 2,520-year timelines. To grasp the significance of these timelines, we must first trace the modern endpoints, which align more as historical periods than singular, fixed events.

Dating the Holocaust and World War II

Not all historians agree about when the Holocaust began. Some argue that it started in January of 1942 with the Wannsee Conference,

---

[90] "The Declaration of the Establishment of the State of Israel." Israel Ministry of Foreign Affairs Website. 2024. www.gov.il. Accessed March 18, 2025. https://www.gov.il/en/pages/declaration-of-establishment-state-of-israel.

where fifteen of the highest-ranking Nazi officials approved the "Final Solution" to the Jewish problem. That "final solution" was the agreement to exterminate all European Jews.[91]

Other historians think the Holocaust began with the invasion of Poland in September 1939, or the annexation of Austria in 1938, since both of those invasions resulted in intense mass persecution of Jews.[92] Still others believe the Holocaust started with the Nuremberg racial purity laws, enacted in Germany in 1935.[93] Some go as far back as 1933 with the rise of the Nazis to power and the burning of the Reichstag as the beginning of the Holocaust.[94][95]

I am not an expert, but I think that the invasion of Poland by Nazi Germany on September 1, 1939, serves as an appropriate marker for the beginning of the Holocaust. Over three million Jews lived in Poland before WWII. In fact, in 1939, more Jews lived in Poland than anywhere else in Europe. According to one online source, almost 90% of Poland's Jewish population died as a result of the Holocaust.[96] Since almost half the Jews who died in the Holocaust came from Poland, it seems to me that the Nazi invasion of Poland in 1939 is a reasonable event in history to mark as the "beginning."

The invasion and annexation of Austria in 1938 could also serve as a starting point for the Holocaust, since there was almost

[91] United States Holocaust Memorial Museum. 2019. "The Wannsee Conference and the 'Final Solution.'" *Holocaust encyclopedia.* Last modified December 8, 2020. Accessed April 11, 2025. https://encyclopedia.ushmm.org/content/en/article/the-wannsee-conference-and-the-final-solution.

[92] United States Holocaust Memorial Museum. 2024. "Timeline of Events." *Holocaust encyclopedia.* Accessed April 9, 2025. https://encyclopedia.ushmm.org/content/en/timeline/holocaust.

[93] Flaws, Jacob. 2025. "The Nuremberg Race Laws." The National WWII Museum | New Orleans. Last modified January 7, 2025. Accessed April 10, 2025. https://www.nationalww2museum.org/war/articles/nuremberg-laws.

[94] United States Holocaust Memorial Museum. 2024. "Timeline of Events." *Holocaust encyclopedia.* Accessed April 9, 2025. https://encyclopedia.ushmm.org/content/en/timeline/holocaust.

[95] My Jewish Learning. 2017. "A Timeline of the Holocaust." My Jewish Learning. Accessed April 9, 2025. https://www.myjewishlearning.com/article/a-timeline-of-the-holocaust/.

[96] Weiner, Rebecca and Mitchell Ward. 2013. "Poland Virtual Jewish History Tour." Jewishvirtuallibrary.org. Last modified January 29, 2025. Accessed April 10, 2025. https://www.jewishvirtuallibrary.org/poland-virtual-jewish-history-tour.

immediately an intense persecution of Jews in Austria following her annexation into Nazi Germany.[97] This annexation was followed by the annexation of the Sudetenland, the occupation of Czechoslovakia, and the Nazi-Soviet non-aggression pact.

The end of the Holocaust is a little easier to date. Most historians use the liberation of the last death camps in May 1945 as the end. I think of the Nuremberg executions in October 1946 as the end of the Holocaust because it was the first formal act of justice taken by the Allied nations against the Nazis. Ten Nazi war criminals were placed on trial for crimes against humanity, and on October 16, 1946, they were hanged for their crimes. Among those war criminals were men who helped orchestrate the "final solution."

A Period of Global Madness

With all this in mind, one can easily argue that the Holocaust lasted at least seven years, from either 1938 to 1945 or 1939 to 1946. The world descended into an insanity of self-destruction. Nations around the world poured massive resources into the mass slaughter of WWII, causing at least 65 million civilian and military deaths. In certain respects, the creation of Israel and her subsequent Declaration of Establishment can be seen as a global desire for a return to a more stable and just world order—a return to sanity.

Having said all this, I'm going to mark 1939 as the beginning of the Holocaust—a time when the world went mad. I will mark 1948, the year of Israel's establishment, as the year when we tried to return to sanity. It is with these markers that I point to the next two prophetic timelines in the book of Daniel. These two historical events form the end dates of our next two timelines.

Daniel 4: The Madness of a King

Daniel 4 is King Nebuchadnezzar's open letter to the world, which he ruled by force and conquest.[98][99] Nebuchadnezzar was a great military commander and builder; his cities, palaces, and

---

[97] United States Holocaust Memorial Museum. n.d. "Nazi Territorial Aggression: The Anschluss." *Holocaust Encyclopedia.* Accessed April 10, 2025. https://encyclopedia.ushmm.org/content/en/article/nazi-territorial-aggression-the-anschluss.

[98] Daniel 4:1-3; 34-37

[99] Daniel 4:33

monuments were renowned throughout the world.[100][101] Yet, as powerful as he was, he was humbled by the Most High God for his arrogance. Daniel 4 is Nebuchadnezzar's autobiographical account of how he was struck with a bout of insanity that lasted seven years, after which he was restored to sanity.

How Long are Seven 'Times'?

According to the story in Daniel 4, Nebuchadnezzar descended into madness for a period of seven 'times.' I want to try and date this period of madness to determine a starting point for our timeline. Four separate verses in Daniel 4 state that King Nebuchadnezzar's madness lasted for seven 'times.'[102] As I wrote previously, I consider a 'time' to be a period of 360 days.

Daniel may provide a hint as to the duration of a 'time' in Daniel 4:29, when he writes, "At the end of twelve months, he (Nebuchadnezzar) walked in the palace of the kingdom of Babylon." The Bible does not say, "after a year;" the specific verbiage is, "at the end of twelve months." I think that this is Daniel's hint that a 'time' is 360 days because 12 months of 30 days is 360 days.

When Did Nebuchadnezzar Go Crazy? When Did the Seven 'Times' Take Place?

Unlike many of the other stories in Daniel, we do not have a specific date for Daniel 4. Neither history nor archaeology have provided us with an account of Nebuchadnezzar's mental illness. In fact, archaeology has very little information about the latter years of Nebuchadnezzar's reign at all.

I base the period of Nebuchadnezzar's madness on the little bit of context that history and the Bible provide. History tells us that the

[100] Muhammed, Shukir. 2016. "Brick Stamped with the Name of Nebuchadnezzar II." *World History Encyclopedia.* Modified June 17, 2016. Accessed April 11, 2025. https://www.worldhistory.org/image/5240/brick-stamped-with-the-name-of-nebuchadnezzar-ii/.
[101] Windle, Bryan. 2019. "Nebuchadnezzar: An Archaeological Biography." *Bible Archaeology Report.* October 17, 2019. Accessed April 10, 2025. https://Biblearchaeologyreport.com/2019/10/17/nebuchadnezzar-an-archaeological-biography/.
[102] Daniel 4:16,23,25 and 32

Babylonians invaded Egypt in 568 or 567 BC. If Nebuchadnezzar was in charge of this invasion, he was sane in 567 BC.[103]

In 573 BC, the city of Tyre surrendered to the Babylonian army after a 13-year siege.[104][105] Tyre probably would not have surrendered if they knew that Nebuchadnezzar was insane. Therefore, Nebuchadnezzar was most likely sane in 573 BC. The final group of Jewish exiles was deported from Jerusalem in 582 BC, a few years after the Babylonian conquest.[106] If this was under Nebuchadnezzar's orders, he was sane enough to give the order.

With all this in mind, I date Nebuchadnezzar's madness to sometime between the deportation of the last exiles in 582 BC and the surrender of Tyre in 573 BC. Sometime during those nine years, Nebuchadnezzar went completely insane for seven 'times' or 2,520 days.

Measuring our 2,520 solar year timeline from 582 BC and 573 BC yields dates ranging from 1939 to 1948. So, Nebuchadnezzar's madness and return to sanity connects to the Holocaust and WWII by a timeline of 2,520 years. Nebuchadnezzar's insanity is linked to a period of global madness in the 20th century by a timeline of 2,520 years.

Daniel 5: The Writing on the Wall and the Nuremberg Executions

Daniel 5 describes the night that Babylon fell to the Persian armies. We know from documents of the time that the fall of Babylon took place on October 12, 539 BC.[107] It was on this night

---

[103] Windle, Bryan. 2022. "Hophra: An Archaeological Biography." *Bible Archaeology Report*. February 4, 2022. Accessed April 10, 2025. https://biblearchaeologyreport.com/2022/02/04/hophra-an-archaeological-biography/..

[104] Dixon, Helen. 2022. "Reexamining Nebuchadnezzar II's 'Thirteen-Year' Siege of Tyre in Phoenician Historiography." *Journal of Ancient History 10 (2): 165–99*. Accessed April 11, 2025. https://doi.org/10.1515/jah-2022-0007.

[105] Britannica editors. 2025. "Tyre." *Encyclopedia Britannica*. Accessed April 10, 2025. https://www.britannica.com/place/Tyre.

[106] Jeremiah 52:30

[107] Radner, Karen and Grant Frame. 2020. *THE ROYAL INSCRIPTIONS OF AMÊL-MARDUK (561–560 BC), NERIGLISSAR (559–556 BC), AND NABONIDUS (555–539 BC), KINGS OF BABYLON: THE ROYAL*

that the last Babylonian king, Belshazzar—grandson of Nebuchadnezzar—threw an enormous party. The night of this party marks the starting date for our timeline.

During this party, in the midst of the revelry, a phantom hand materialized out of thin air and began writing an encrypted message on the plaster of the banquet room's wall.[108] At first, no one could decipher the writing on the wall.

It took some time, but eventually, the prophet Daniel,—one of Nebuchadnezzar's former advisors—was able to decipher the words on the wall. Daniel pronounced the mysterious words and then declared the meaning of each word.

The words on the wall were *MENE, MENE, TEKEL, UPHARSIN*. Daniel interpreted the message for Belshazzar and all who were in the banquet room. Belshazzar had been weighed and found wanting, his kingdom was about to be taken from him and divided by his enemies.[109]

Daniel's prophetic interpretation of the words was fulfilled that very evening. The armies of the Medes and Persians conquered Babylon that night.

Each word in the message carries an additional meaning related to Hebrew weights. Mene also means Mina, equivalent to a weight of 50 Shekels or 1,000 Gerahs. Tekel also means Shekel, which is a weight of one Shekel or 20 Gerahs. Upharsin, or Parsin, is equivalent to a half-Mina, a weight of 500 Gerahs.[110] These weights, when combined—Mina (1,000 Gerahs), Mina (1,000 Gerahs), Shekel (20 Gerahs), Parsin (500 Gerahs)—add up to a total of 2,520 Gerahs.[111]

INSCRIPTIONS OF THE NEO-BABYLONIAN EMPIRE. University Park, Pennsylvania. Pennsylvania State University. Pg 26

[108] Daniel 5:5

[109] Daniel 5:25-28

[110] Barker, Kenneth L, and Donald W Burdick. 1995. *The NIV Study Bible*. Grand Rapids, Mi: Zondervan Pub. House. 1299 margin notes; Table of Weights and Measures 1953

[111] "What Do the Words Mene, Mene, Tekel, Upharsin Mean (Daniel 5:25)?" n.d. www.cgg.org. Accessed November 2, 2022. https://www.cgg.org/index.cfm/library/bqa/id/65/what-do-words-mene-mene-tekel-upharsin-mean-daniel-525.htm.

2520 Bookended by 73 years and 73 Days

The timeline in this calculation is bookended by the destruction of Jewish enemies, both ancient and modern. It is further bookended by a period in the ancient past of 73 years, which is mirrored by 73 days in 1946.

Babylon defeated Assyria in 612 BC by destroying the Assyrian capital city of Nineveh. Seventy-three years after the destruction of Nineveh, Babylon fell to the armies of Cyrus the Great in 539 BC.[112] For 73 years, the Neo-Babylonian Empire was the global superpower.

Daniel intended this timeline to be understood as 2,520 'times.' Counting 907,200 days into the future from October 12, 539 BC, arrives on August 5, 1946.[113]

August 5, 1946, was during the Nuremberg trials. Ten Nazi war criminals were hanged 73 days later, on October 16, 1946. Those 73 days in 1946 are linked symbolically and prophetically to the 73 years that the Neo-Babylonian empire reigned supreme, from 612 BC to 539 BC.

An in-depth analysis of the embedded numbers in Daniel 5 is available in Appendix III of this book.

Connecting Jeremiah to the Holocaust

Jeremiah 42 recounts events that took place after the destruction of Jerusalem in 586 BC.[114] These events occurred either in 586 BC or a few years later, in 582 BC; scholars disagree on the dates.[115] These two years serve as starting points for our timelines. I think it is more likely that the events in Jeremiah 41-42 took place in 582 BC, but I will examine both dates.

---

[112] Saggs, H.W. 2000. "Babylon." *Encyclopedia Britannica.* Last modified March 18, 2025. Accessed April 10, 2025. https://www.britannica.com/place/Babylon-ancient-city-Mesopotamia-Asia.

[113] August 5, 1946, coincides with the Jewish day of mourning Tisha B'Av 1946. A date associated with the destruction of Jerusalem in 586 BC and AD 70.

[114] Thiele, Edwin R. 2004. *The Mysterious Numbers of the Hebrew Kings.* Grand Rapids, Mi: Kregel. 187.

[115] Barker, Kenneth L., and John R. Kohlenberger. *Zondervan NIV Bible Commentary, vol. 1: Old Testament* Grand Rapids, Mich: Zondervan, 1994. 1245.

Background

The Babylonian army destroyed Jerusalem in 586 BC. Judah's army was destroyed, and the Temple was looted and burned to the ground. Many of Judah's educated and leadership class were taken captive to Babylon. The final exile of Jewish leadership occurred in 582 BC.[116] This loss of the nation's leadership created a power vacuum in Judah.

The Babylonians filled this leadership vacuum by appointing leaders in Judah. Babylon appointed Gedaliah as governor over Judah. Though he attempted to lead the people, he was assassinated by political rivals soon after being put in charge.[117] After his death, the country descended into even greater chaos.

By the time of Gedaliah's assassination, Jeremiah had joined the survivors of Jerusalem's destruction and had begun to minister to them as prophet.

One of the remaining officers of the army, Johanan, stepped forward to lead the remnant of Jewish survivors. Johanan, along with some of the remnant of Judah's destruction, approached Jeremiah for advice as to whether they should flee to Egypt.

Jeremiah counseled the people not to flee to Egypt. The worst was over, and God promised to protect whoever remained in Judah.

God's statement through Jeremiah was clear. Do not go to Egypt.

The LORD hath said concerning you, O ye remnant of Judah; Go ye not into Egypt: know certainly that I have admonished you this day." Jeremiah 42:19

There are five nouns in this short verse warning the remaining Jews to stay in Judah. The noun frequency values, and their translations are in the table on the next page. When multiplied together, those noun frequency values equal 2,520. There are 2,520 years between the death of Gedaliah and the modern Holocaust.

---

[116] Jeremiah 52:30
[117] Jeremiah 41:1-7

Noun	Hebrew	Strong's	Occurrence
LORD	יהוה	H3068	20
Remnant	שארית	H7611	3
Judah	יהודה	H3063	2
Egypt	מצרים	H4714	7
Day	יום	H3117	3

We must infer the dates in Jeremiah 42 from what we know about the events recounted in Jeremiah 41 and 42. The assassination of Gedaliah took place either in 586 BC or 582 BC.[118] Traditionally, Gedaliah's death is commemorated by observant Jews as a minor day of fasting each year on the third day of the fall month of Tishri. Tradition holds that this is when Gedaliah was murdered.

Based on the large number of events that took place between the destruction of Jerusalem and the death of Gedaliah, it seems more likely to me that his assassination happened in 582 BC. Nevertheless, I will include calculations for both 582 BC and 586 BC. Each calculation reveals interesting results.

The fall month of Tishri 582 BC began on September 23; therefore, the third day of Tishri (the fast of Gedaliah) was September 25, 582 BC.[119] We will use this as our precise starting date for this timeline.

If we measure 2,520 solar years from September 25, 582 BC, we arrive on September 17, 1939. Nazi Germany invaded Poland on September 1, 1939. The Soviet Union followed suit on September 17, invading Poland from the east. The invasion of Poland started WWII and sealed the doom of Polish Jews living there.

The invasion of Poland was the trigger that started WWII. It also began Nazi efforts to exterminate more than three million Jewish people living in Poland. If the death of Gedaliah took place in Tishri of 582 BC, we have a precise timeline of 2,520 solar years connecting his death to the beginning of WWII in September 1939. We can also

---

[118] Barker, Kenneth L., and John R. Kohlenberger. *Zondervan NIV Bible Commentary, vol. 1: Old Testament* Grand Rapids, Mich: Zondervan, 1994. 1245.

[119] Parker, Richard A, and Waldo H Dubberstein. 2007. *Babylonian Chronology 626 B.C.- A.D. 75*. Eugene, Or.: Wipf & Stock. 28. Seventh month began 9/23; 3rd day was 9/25.

date the beginning of the Holocaust to that month. Both the Holocaust and WWII are mentioned prominently in the Declaration of Establishment.

What About 586 BC; What if Gedaliah was Assassinated Immediately After the Temple Burned?

If we begin our timeline in 586 BC, we get interesting results as well. In the year 586 BC, Tishri began on October 7. The fast of Gedaliah would have been on October 9, 586 BC.[120] Counting 2,520 solar years, or 920,409 days, into the future brings us to October 1, 1935. This was two weeks after the Nuremberg Laws were signed in Nazi Germany. The laws were first written on September 15, promulgated on September 16, and put in force almost immediately.[121]

As I wrote before, there are some disagreements about precisely when to date the beginning of the Holocaust. Both the invasion of Poland in 1939 and the Nuremberg racial purity laws in 1935, are universally recognized as important milestones on any timeline of the Holocaust.

Regardless of whether the assassination of Gedaliah took place in 586 BC or 582 BC, the timeline yields profound results that cannot be easily ignored. It is particularly striking that these timelines link both dates to modern events explicitly mentioned in the Declaration of Establishment.

The Lessons of Jeremiah 42

Ninety percent of the Jewish people living in Poland were murdered by the Nazis during WWII.[122][123] This genocide began in

---

[120] Parker, Richard A, and Waldo H Dubberstein. 2007. *Babylonian Chronology 626 B.C.- A.D. 75*. Eugene, Or.: Wipf & Stock. 28.

[121] Bradsher, Greg. 2010. "The Nuremberg Laws." *Prologue Magazine*. 2010. Last updated April 2023. Accessed April 10, 2025. The U.S. National Archives and Records Administration.
https://www.archives.gov/publications/prologue/2010/winter/nuremberg.html.

[122] Vashem, Yad. 2019. "Murder of the Jews of Poland | Www.yadvashem.org." Yadvashem.org. 2019. Accessed April 10, 2025.
https://www.yadvashem.org/holocaust/about/fate-of-jews/poland.html.

[123] Jewish Virtual Library. 2019. "Estimated Number of Jews Killed in the Final Solution." Jewishvirtuallibrary.org. Accessed April 10, 2025.

September 1939, exactly 2,520 years after the events in Jeremiah 42 took place. Jews in antiquity and Jews living in 20th-century Europe discovered the same truth—they were not safe among Gentiles.

In 582 BC, the LORD admonished the Jewish remnant not to flee to a foreign country for safety. They ignored the LORD and fled to Egypt anyway. They were seeking safety, but they encountered destruction. Around 567 BC, the Babylonian army invaded Egypt. The Babylonian army passed through Judah without incident, but they invaded Egypt through the very areas where the Jewish people had tried to settle down. Less than twenty years after the destruction of Jerusalem, the Jewish remnant faced Babylonian invaders again.

The tragic history of the Jewish people reveals that, no matter how safe they feel in a foreign land, that safety is only temporary. Eventually, things always go bad. That is the lesson of Jeremiah 42; that is the lesson of the Jewish people in Poland in 1939; and that is the lesson for the world today.

The Jewish people can only hope for long-term safety in their own land.

---

https://www.jewishvirtuallibrary.org/estimated-number-of-jews-killed-in-the-final-solution.

Chapter Eight

UN Resolution 181, 2,520 and the Creation of Israel

*On the 29th of November, 1947, the United Nations General
Assembly passed a resolution calling for the establishment of a
Jewish State in Eretz-Israel; the General Assembly required
the inhabitants of Eretz-Israel to take such steps as were
necessary on their part for the implementation of that resolution.
This recognition by the United Nations of the right of the
Jewish people to establish their State is irrevocable.*[124]

Paragraph eight of the Declaration of Establishment provides
the end-date for this timeline. The United Nations adopted
Resolution 181 on November 29, 1947.[125] This resolution provided
for the partition of Mandatory Palestine into separate independent
states—one Jewish, one Arab. Essentially, UN Resolution 181 is the
order that created the modern state of Israel.

The immediate effect of this resolution for people living in
Mandatory Palestine was conflict. Almost immediately, Palestinian
Arabs attacked their Jewish neighbors. Arab militias began an open
campaign of guerrilla warfare against Jewish settlers. These militias
gained covert military assistance from neighboring Arab states. Once
Israel declared her independence in 1948, these same Arab states
declared war and invaded. Though severely outnumbered, the nation
of Israel emerged victorious in what is now known as the First Arab-
Israeli War, or, alternately, Israel's War for Independence.[126][127]

Daniel contains two chapters linked to 1947 by timelines of
2,520 'times.'

[124] "The Declaration of the Establishment of the State of Israel." 2024. www.gov.il.
2024. Accessed April 10, 2025. https://www.gov.il/en/pages/declaration-of-
establishment-state-of-israel. Paragraph eight.
[125] Jewish Virtual Library. n.d. "UN General Assembly Resolution 181." n.d.
www.jewishvirtuallibrary.org. Accessed April 10, 2025.
https://www.jewishvirtuallibrary.org/un-general-assembly-resolution-181-2.
[126] Karsh, Efraim. 2008. *The Arab-Israeli Conflict: The 1948 War.* New York: Rosen
Pub. Kindle Edition.
[127] Safran, Nadav. 1982. *Israel: The Embattled Ally.* Cambridge, Mass.; London: The
Belknap Press of Harvard University Press. 43.

November 29, 1947: The Day After 252 Days Had Passed in the Year

UN Resolution 181 was adopted on November 29, 1947. This marks the end-date for our timeline. The Jewish calendar is lunisolar; as a result, the first day of each year varies from year to year. In 1947, the Jewish calendar began on March 22nd. November 29, 1947, was the 253rd day of the Jewish calendar that year. In other words, **252** days passed in 1947 and then, the very next day, Resolution 181 was adopted.[128][129]

If this were not an odd enough coincidence, the digits that compose the year 1947 (1, 9, 4, and 7), when multiplied together, equal **252.**

In base-60 numbers, **252** is expressed as $4,12_{base60}$: four in the 60s column (240) plus 12 in the units column. There are 907,200 days in 2,520 years of 360 days each. In base-60 numbers, 907,200 and 252 are closely associated. The longer number **907,200** is calculated as **$252 * 60^2$**. Written in base-60 numbers, **252 is $4,12_{base60}$**, which closely resembles **$4,12,0,0_{base60}$** (907,200). The ancient Babylonians wrote both numbers as ￼.

The Number 907,200 in Daniel 6

Daniel 6 recounts the story of Daniel in the lion's den. In the original Aramaic manuscripts, however, the story begins in Daniel 5:31 with the verse, "And Darius the Median took the kingdom, being about threescore and two years old." This is significant because it influences the embedded equations in Daniel 6.

The marginal notes in some Bibles annotate the fact that the first verse for this story was originally 5:31. The online resource, Blue Letter Bible includes a note stating that the Westminster Leningrad

---

[128] HebCal. n.d. "Jewish Calendar 1947 Diaspora - Hebcal." Hebcal.com. Accessed April 11, 2025.
https://www.hebcal.com/hebcal?year=1947&v=1&yt=G&nx=on&o=on&d=on&c=off&maj=on&min=on&mod=on&mf=off&ss=off.
[129] "Julian Day and Date Time Calculator." n.d. Www.csgnetwork.com. Accessed April 11, 2025. http://www.csgnetwork.com/juliandaydate.html. All timelines were measured with this tool.

Codex, one of the oldest Hebrew Bibles in existence, numbers the verses of the story beginning with verse 5:31.[130]

With that in mind, we will look at our first calculation:

> *It pleased Darius to set over the kingdom an hundred and twenty princes, which should be over the whole kingdom; And over these three presidents; of whom Daniel was first: that the princes might give accounts unto them, and the king should have no damage. Daniel 6:1-2*

Daniel was placed at the head of all the princes. 'Daniel' occurs 21 times in the chapter. When we multiply 120 'princes' (120) times 'Daniel' (21) we get 2,520. 120*21=2,520.

*120 princes (120) * Daniel (21)*

*120*21=2,520*

Now let's examine Daniel 6:1-2 with the frequency values inserted in the text. Notice that 'prince' is specifically enumerated as 120. There were 120 'princes.' There were three 'presidents.' All other nouns are quantified based solely on the number of times they occurred in the original Aramaic.

> *It pleased Darius **(6)** to set over the kingdom **(10)** an hundred and twenty **(120)** princes, which should be over the whole kingdom; And over these three **(3)** presidents; of whom Daniel **(21)** was first **(2)**. Daniel 6:1-2*

Consistent with calculations throughout the book of Daniel, any particular noun is only multiplied once,[131] regardless of how many times that noun occurs in a particular verse. The word 'kingdom' is stated twice here, but it is only multiplied once. If we multiply these values, we get:

*Darius (6) * kingdom (10) * princes (120) * presidents (3) * Daniel (21) * first (2)*

907,200 or 4,12,0,0$_{base60}$

---

[130] Blue Letter Bible. https://www.blueletterBible.org/kjv/dan/5/31/s_855031.
[131] Lester, Mike. 2024. *2520: The Hidden Key in the Book of Daniel*. First. Independently Published. 38, 115.

The story in Daniel 6 is about the 'king' (24) who cast 'Daniel' (21) into the 'den of lions' (5). Multiplied together, these values equal 2,520, $42,0_{base60}$. The compound noun 'den of lions' occurs five times in the chapter. 'King' in all forms, occurs 31 times. As a common noun, 'king' appears 24 times; as the honorific, "O King" it occurs seven times. Here 'king' is a common noun and receives the value of 24. 'Daniel' as we previously mentioned, occurs 21 times.

King (24) * Daniel (21) * den of lions (5) equals

2,520 or $42,0_{base60}$.

These patterns emerge repeatedly in Daniel 6. In the interest of brevity, however, I am only going to show one more calculation. If you are interested in more detail, *2520: The Hidden Key in the Book of Daniel* contains additional embedded calculations.[132]

Daniel 6:3

Then this Daniel was preferred above the presidents and princes, because an excellent spirit was in him; and the king thought to set him over the whole realm. Daniel 6:3

Word	Occurrence
Daniel	21
Presidents	5
Princes	6
Spirit	1
King	24 or 31
Set (*qum*) verb	6
Realm (kingdom)	10

Calculations Include Verbs and Nouns, and Nouns Only

This calculation also uses the verb, "to set," or "to set up." It is difficult to know if Daniel intended to use the verb, so I include calculations with the verb and with nouns only.

Word Values Are Based on Original Language Not on KJV

The Aramaic word *Malkut* 'kingdom,' occurs ten times in the story, from Daniel 5:31-6:28; so, 'kingdom' is assigned a value of 10. This word is translated three different ways in the King James

[132] Lester, Mike. 2024. 113-132.

Version of the Bible. The Aramaic word *malkut*, can mean "realm," or "kingdom," or "reign."[133] *Malkut* occurs twice as "reign," in 6:28; it occurs once as "realm," in 6:3. *Malkut* occurs once as "kingdom" in 5:31 and six times as "kingdom" in the rest of Daniel 6. The frequency value is assigned based on the **original language**, not on its English translation in the King James Version.

'Princes' and 'presidents' are not explicitly enumerated in this verse, as they were in the preceding verse. Therefore, their values are determined by frequency of occurrence. 'Prince' appears six times in the story; 'president' appears five times. 'King' occurs a total of 31 times: seven times as an honorific ("O king") and 24 times as a common noun. In this verse, it is a common noun and is assigned the value of 24.

Daniel (21) * president (5) * prince (six) *king (24) *set over (6) * kingdom (10)

$$21*5*6*24*6*10 = 907,200 \text{ or } 4,12,0,0_{base60}$$

Calculated with nouns only the result is:

151,200 or 42,0,0$_{base60}$

It is important to notice the base-60 expression in this final equation. The number 151,200 divided by 60 is 2,520. It is the same as 42*60*60; or 42,0,0$_{base60}$.

Babylonians, during Daniel's day, wrote the numbers 42, 2,520, and 151,200 in the exact same way: 𒌋𒌋 𒁹 .[134] As odd as it may seem to a Western eye, the ancient Babylonians used context to distinguish the difference between these numbers. Daniel took advantage of this ambiguity in his embedded equations, using these numbers the way a writer might use a homonym or homograph.

To an ancient Babylonian in the 6th century BC, the numbers 151,200 and 2,520 probably would have seemed synonymous, or seemed linked, since they were expressed visually with the same sign:

---

[133] Double quotations indicate the word as quoted from the English text. Single quotation denotes the English translation of a word as it occurred in Hebrew or Aramaic.
[134] "Babylonian Numerals Converter - Online Number System Calculator." 2015. Dcode.fr. Accessed April 10, 2025. https://www.dcode.fr/babylonian-numbers.

⪦ ∏. Likewise, 907,200 was likely seen as synonymous with 252, since both were written: ⊤ ⟨ ∏.[135]

If you are interested in checking my work, there is a very helpful conversion tool on the website: https://www.dcode.fr/babylonian-numbers. The DCode website contains a large number of tools for hobbyist cryptographers, but they also have several conversion tools for ancient number systems, such as Mayan and Egyptian, and Babylonian.

Connecting Daniel 6 to the Creation of Israel November 29, 1947

Daniel 6 was written during the first year of Darius, which began in 538 BC. The Babylonian calendar in 538 BC began on March 24.[136] When we count from March 24, 538 BC, into the future 907,200 days, we arrive on January 15, 1947 AD.[137] This was the same year the UN adopted Resolution 181. This is not as accurate as some of our other calculations. However, we do not know which day in 538 BC Daniel was thrown to the lions, so we are left to speculate about the precise day to start our timeline.

As I mentioned earlier, November 29, 1947—the date that the United Nations adopted Resolution 181, creating Israel—was the day after 252 days had passed in the Jewish calendar year in 1947. The number **252** in base-60 is $4,12_{base60}$. This is obviously related to **907,200**, which is $4,12,0,0_{base60}$. Both of these numbers, when written in Babylonian, look like this: ⊤ ⟨ ∏.

So, $4,12,0,0_{base60}$ (907,200) days passed from the first year of Darius to the year 1947. In that year, on the 253rd day of the Jewish calendar, the United Nations adopted Resolution 181, creating Israel. This was the day after a total of $4,12_{base60}$ (252) days had passed in the Jewish year.

[135] "Babylonian Numerals Converter - Online Number System Calculator." 2015. Dcode.fr. Accessed April 10, 2025. https://www.dcode.fr/babylonian-numbers.
[136] Parker, Richard A, and Waldo H Dubberstein. 2007. *Babylonian Chronology 626 B.C.- A.D. 75*. Eugene, Or.: Wipf & Stock. 29.
[137] "Julian Day and Date Time Calculator." n.d. www.csgnetwork.com. Accessed April 11, 2025. http://www.csgnetwork.com/juliandaydate.html.

So, when written in Babylonian numbers, we have a timeline of 𒁹 𒌋 𒐖 [138]days reaching the year 1947 and 𒁹 𒌋 𒐖 [139] days within 1947. The digits of the year 1947 multiply to equal 252 or 𒁹 𒌋 𒐖 .

The timeline number seems to represent a time of waiting, a time that the Jewish people were in exile in the nations. It is almost as if, once this time had expired, they were destined to return to the land.

Parallels Between 538 BC and 1947

There are some interesting historical parallels between the events of 538 BC and 1947 AD. In 538 BC, the Gentile king Cyrus the Great, issued a decree that the Jewish people should return to Jerusalem to rebuild the city and the temple.[140] Similarly, in 1947, the Gentile United Nations adopted a resolution permitting the Jewish people to return to their homeland. When the exiles returned in 538 BC to rebuild the temple, they met resistance from people who were already living there;[141] likewise, in 1947, the Jewish people returning to Israel also faced resistance from local populations.[142]

In both cases, an enemy of the Jewish people had recently been defeated by a Gentile army. In 539 BC, the allied Medes and Persians conquered Babylon; in 1945, the Allied forces of the United States, Soviet Union, and Great Britain defeated Nazi Germany. In each case, the Jewish people appeared broken and defeated. Both returns to the promised land had been foretold in the Bible.

Daniel 9 is also dated to the first year of Darius. That chapter has an embedded instance of the number 2,520. This next timeline connects directly to the date of the Declaration of Establishment itself, May 14, 1948.

---

[138] 907,200 days
[139] 252 days
[140] Ezra 1:1-4
[141] Ezra 4:1-4
[142] Safran, Nadav. 1982. *Israel—the Embattled Ally*. Harvard University Press. 43-44.

Chapter Nine

Daniel 9, 2,520, and the Independence of Israel 1948

...and the end thereof shall be with a flood, and unto the end of the war desolations are determined. Daniel 9:26b

וקצו בשטף ועד קץ מלחמה נחרצת שממות:

This final timeline connects the signing date of the Declaration of Establishment, May 14, 1948, to the Messianic prophecy in Daniel 9. This timeline consists of 2,520 'times' plus 69 literal weeks. This chronologically specific timeline includes numbers embedded in the text of Daniel 9 and is dated based on Daniel 9:1, beginning with the first year of Darius in 538 BC.

Daniel 9 contains a chronologically specific Messianic prophecy that has fascinated Bible scholars for centuries. The angel Gabriel introduced the prophecy with the statement, "Seventy weeks have been determined for your people and your holy city" (Daniel 9:24). The most common interpretation of these seventy weeks is that they represent weeks of years. Gabriel divided the seventy weeks into periods of 7 weeks, 62 weeks (69 weeks), and one final week.

So, the prophecy, in its total timeline, is often understood as either 490 years (70 weeks of years) or as 483 years, with a final seven-year period interpreted in various ways. Since Gabriel introduced the prophecy as "Seventy Weeks," it has become known popularly as the "Seventy Weeks Prophecy."

This divine timeline anticipating the arrival of the Messiah has been interpreted many times by scholars and theologians far more qualified than me. I cannot add much to the Messianic aspect of this prophecy, and do not intend to. What I offer here is a look at additional aspects of the Daniel 9 prophecy that are sometimes overlooked.

The simplest understanding of the prophecy indicates that before the final seven-year period can take place, the Jewish people must return to their homeland. In fact, they did return to their homeland twice: first in 537 BC after Cyrus's decree in 538 BC; and then in 1948 AD. In this chapter, I will show how Gabriel's timeline relates to both of those returns.

Hebrew Numbers and Daniel 9:26

The number system of the ancient Hebrews was closely tied to their written language. Each letter of the Hebrew alphabet was assigned a numerical value. The first nine letters represented the values one through nine. The next nine letters represented the values 10, 20, 30, and so on, through 90. The final four letters represented the values 100, 200, 300, and 400. These letters were added together to represent a total value.

This close relationship between letters and numbers in the Hebrew system meant that words, and even phrases, could hold numerical values based on the letters that composed them. An entire field of Hebrew mysticism has evolved around this phenomenon; however, I will not delve into that here.

Daniel 9:26: Seven Words with the Value 2,520

Yakov Rambsel, in his book *The Genesis Factor*, demonstrated that the final seven words in Daniel 9:26 hold the value 2,520 when observed as Hebrew numbers.[143] When all the letters of these seven words are added together, their combined sum is 2,520. These seven words lead into Gabriel's description of a final seven-year period of war and desolations still awaiting Jerusalem and the Holy Land.

The fact that the Hebrew words in the final clause of Daniel 9:26 add up to 2,520 could potentially be dismissed as a coincidence, except that the following verse, Daniel 9:27, specifically references a week of years.

> *And he shall confirm the covenant with many for one week: and in the midst of the week he shall cause the sacrifice and the oblation to cease, and for the overspreading of abominations he shall make it desolate, even until the consummation, and that determined shall be poured upon the desolate. Daniel 9:27*

---

[143] Rambsel, Yacov A. 2000. *The Genesis Factor: The Amazing Mysteries of the Bible Codes.* Beverly Hills, Ca: Lion's Head Pub. Pg 186.

I think Daniel intended this figurative week of years to be understood as seven 'times' of 360 days each, or a total of 2,520 days.

Take a look at the tables below to see the numbers and their final sum.

Daniel 9:26 Interlinear English Hebrew

Desolations	Are determined	Of the war	The end	And unto	Shall be with a flood	And the end
שממות	נחרצת	מלחמה	קץ	ועד	בשטף	וקצו
786	748	123	190	80	391	202

To better understand Rambsel's findings, we should examine the next table, which gives a letter-by-letter break-down of the Hebrew numbers for the final seven words of Daniel 9:26. Hopefully, this table provides a better sense of how the value 2,520 is obtained by adding each letter's numerical equivalent.

Daniel 9:26 Hebrew Letters with Numerical Values Beneath

ד	ע	ו	ף	ט	ש	ב	ו	צ	ק	ו
4	70	6	80	9	300	2	6	90	100	6
צ	ר	ח	נ	ה	מ	ח	ל	מ	ץ	ק
90	200	8	50	5	40	8	30	40	90	100
					ת	ו	מ	מ	ש	ת
					400	6	40	40	300	400

These seven words in Daniel 9:26 precede the discussion in 9:27 about the final week of history in which a covenant is made "for one week." This week is best understood as a week of years. The last seven words of 9:26 anticipates this week of years by embedding 2,520 into the numerical value of the Hebrew words themselves.

The preceding verse, Daniel 9:25, specifies that a period of 69 weeks will follow a decree to restore Jerusalem. These 69 'weeks' are normally understood as periods of seven years. However, for the next couple of paragraphs, I am going to examine the interesting ways that the number 69 is connected to the first return of the exiles to Jerusalem during Daniel's lifetime.

The Sixty-Ninth Year After Daniel.

The number 69 turns out to have a couple of interesting fulfillments in the lives of the Jewish exiles during Daniel's lifetime. The book of Daniel begins in the third year of Jehoiakim, September 19, 606 BC.[144][145] Jehoiakim was the king of Judah; his regnal years began in the fall. Sixty-nine years after this, or, alternatively, 70 years of 360 days each, arrives on or about Yom Kippur, September 537 BC.[146] According to *The Zondervan NIV Commentary*, this would have been in exactly the same month that the first Jewish exiles returned to Jerusalem from captivity after Cyrus the Great's decree of 538 BC.[147]

Cyrus' decree stated:

> *Thus saith Cyrus king of Persia, The LORD God of heaven hath given me all the kingdoms of the earth; and he hath charged me to build him an house at Jerusalem, which is in Judah. Who is there among you of all his people? his God be with him, and let him go up to Jerusalem, which is in Judah, and build the house of the LORD God of Israel, (he is the God,) which is in Jerusalem. Ezra 1:2-3*

So, the life of Daniel seems to have been intertwined with the fate of his people, because it was in the seventh month of 537 BC that the Babylonian exiles first returned to Jerusalem, rebuilt and consecrated the altar, and observed the holy days of the seventh

---

[144] Daniel 1:1

[145] Parker, Richard A, and Waldo H Dubberstein. 2007. *Babylonian Chronology 626 B.C.- A.D. 75*. Eugene, Or.: Wipf & Stock. 27.

[146]"Julian Day and Date Time Calculator." n.d. www.csgnetwork.com. Accessed April 11, 2025. http://www.csgnetwork.com/juliandaydate.html.

[147] Barker, Kenneth L., and John R. Kohlenberger. *Zondervan NIV Bible Commentary, vol. 1: Old Testament*. Grand Rapids, Mich: Zondervan, 1994. 683 and 685

month.[148] There were 69 years from the date at the beginning of the book of Daniel to the first return of the exiles in 537 BC.[149][150]

Sixty-nine Weeks and Sixty-nine Days After the First Year of Darius

Sixty-nine literal weeks of 24-hour days has an interesting fulfillment as well in relation to the first return. Daniel 9:1 is dated to the first year of Darius,[151] which began in Nisanu 538 BC, or March 24, 538 BC.[152] Gabriel gave a timeline of sixty-nine weeks as a part of his prophecy to Daniel. Counting 483 days (69 literal weeks) from March 24, 538 BC, arrives on July 19, 537 BC. This was the 49-year anniversary of the breaching of the walls of Jerusalem and capture of King Zedekiah in 586 BC.[153][154]

So, in September of 537 BC, the returning exiles were beginning the fiftieth year after they had lost their land, their city, their temple, and their king. While we have no confirmation that 537 BC was an actual jubilee year, it was certainly figuratively a jubilee, as there was a literal return of the captives to their land.[155]

The number 69 has one more interesting fulfillment in the lives of the exiles in 537 BC. The last day of the Feast of Tabernacles in 537 BC—the holy day known as Hoshana Rabba—was September 26, 537 BC.[156] This was 552 days

---

[148] Ezra 3:1-6

[149] Ezra 3:1-6

[150] Barker, Kenneth L, and Donald W Burdick. 1995. *The NIV Study Bible*. Grand Rapids, Mi: Zondervan Pub. House. Pg 669 marginal notes.

[151] Daniel 9:1

[152] Parker, Richard A, and Waldo H Dubberstein. 2007. *Babylonian Chronology 626 B.C.- A.D. 75*. Eugene, Or.: Wipf & Stock. 29.

[153] Thiele, Edwin R. 2004. *The Mysterious Numbers of the Hebrew Kings*. Grand Rapids, Mi: Kregel. 184 and 189.

[154] Jeremiah 52:6-11

[155] Isaiah 61:1

[156] Parker, Richard A, and Waldo H Dubberstein. 2007. Pg 29.

after March 24, 538 BC, the date in Daniel 9:1.[157] This 18-month period of 552 days is 69 weeks plus 69 days.

So, the number 69 reoccurs in the life of Daniel and the exiles in a couple of ways. The exiles returned **69 literal years** (25,202 days) after the date of Daniel 1:1. Additionally, the first returned exiles to Jerusalem completed their observation of the Feast of Tabernacles **69 weeks and 69 days** after the date of Daniel 9.

Connecting Daniel 9 to the 20th Century; 2,520 'Times' Plus 69 Weeks May 1948

Daniel 9:1 is dated to the first year of Darius, March 24, 538 BC. The number 2,520, embedded in the numerical values in the text of Daniel 9:26, is seven years of 360 days, or seven 'times.' If these days prophetically represent years, then we have 2,520 'times' or 907,200 days.

Counting forward **907,200** days from March 24, 538 BC, we arrive on January 15, 1947.[158] We already established this in our analysis of Daniel 6. Daniel 9 is a bit different, though, since there is heavy emphasis on the 69 weeks. If we add **69 weeks**, or **483 literal days**, to 907,200 days we get 907,683 days. Measuring **907,683** days from the date of Daniel 9:1, we arrive on May 12, 1948—just two days before the Declaration of Establishment of the State of Israel was signed.[159]

Parallels Between 538 BC and AD 1947

The parallels are striking between the events of 538 BC and AD 1947. In each case, the Jewish people had been living in exile and dreamed of a return. In each case, Gentile alliances had defeated Jewish enemies. In 538 BC, the Medes and Persians had just defeated the Babylonians; in AD 1947, the Allied powers had just defeated the Nazis. In each case,

---

[157] Parker, Richard A, and Waldo H Dubberstein. 2007.. Pg 29.
[158] "Julian Day and Date Time Calculator." 2025. csgnetwork.com. Accessed April 10, 2025. http://www.csgnetwork.com/juliandaydate.html#google_vignette.
[159] "The Declaration of the Establishment of the State of Israel." 2024. Israel Ministry of Foreign Affairs. www.gov.il. 2024. Accessed April 10, 2025. https://www.gov.il/en/pages/declaration-of-establishment-state-of-israel.

Gentile powers encouraged the return of exiled Jews to Palestine. In 538 BC, it was the decree of Cyrus. In 1947, it was the United Nations Resolution 181. In each case, there were people already living in the land who tried to prevent the rebuilding of a Jewish nation. In each case, the Jewish people appeared broken and defeated, without remedy. Finally, each return was predicted in the Bible.

At this point, it seems obvious that there was a supernatural hand at work when the Bible was created. The embedded numbers in some of these prophecies apparently anticipated important dates in modern Jewish history, including the independence of modern Israel.

Chapter Ten

Final Thoughts

Did I Keep my Promises?

In the introduction to this book, I promised to show plain, incontrovertible evidence that the Bible has a supernatural origin. I promised to reveal timelines embedded in the text of the Bible that connect to the modern state of Israel. I promised to show numbers—numbers easily seen, counted, added, and multiplied. I promised to demonstrate how those timelines touch the modern state of Israel and, in fact, connect to five events named in Israel's Declaration of Establishment.

As the reader, you must be the final judge, but I believe I have kept those promises. In the five main chapters of this book, I provided brief backgrounds on the historical events and personalities mentioned in the Declaration, along with their associated dates. I then highlighted specific passages of scripture that parallel modern events, including the dates of those passages. Each of these passages of scripture contains timelines that connect the dates of scripture to the events and personalities mentioned in the Declaration.

I do not know any natural explanation of how so many apparent timelines in scripture could connect to specific dates in history with such accuracy. One or two instances showing time-specific links could be dismissed as coincidence or blind luck. This is more than half-a-dozen. It should be impossible for this to occur.

What Does This Mean?

Daniel and Jeremiah both declared that they received their information from God, the creator and ruler of the heavens and the earth. I believe them.

So, what does all this mean?

- There is a God.
- He is not us.
- He apparently is deeply involved in and concerned about human affairs. He cares about humanity.

- The Bible is a communication from God, containing truths from God in the plain text. Those truths can be understood by humanity. However, the Bible has been constructed in a way that is mysterious and not completely comprehensible to the human mind. As a result, the Bible will always be worthy of more study.
- Every word in the Bible counts. The way the words are organized is important.
- The Bible has been passed to us accurately in its present form. None of these embedded equations could exist if someone had altered the text significantly over the past 2,000 years.
- Modern Israel is a providential nation. In other words, Israel exists because God wants Israel to exist.
- God cares a great deal about what happens to the Jewish people and the nation of Israel.

In the introduction to this book, I promised that, as the reader, you would never approach the Bible or modern Israel in quite the same way again. I hope that promise has been fulfilled for you.

There is something about the Bible. There is a plainspoken aspect to the narratives and poetry that is accessible to readers of all ages and backgrounds. There is something incomprehensibly eternal in the pages of the Bible as well. There is something mysterious and profound. Ultimately, this is why the Bible continues to hold the attention of so many people, even today.

It is my deepest hope that you will approach the Bible with a newfound sense of awe and curiosity. If you have read my book once, give it to your friends and family. There is no point in reading it again, and no point in your friends buying their own copy.

Read the Bible daily; read it deeply. Hold to it as though it were your most treasured possession. I believe the treasures of wisdom found in scripture can change the world for the better.

A Bit About Current Events in Our Nation

I must address current events in our nation as they concern modern Israel and this most recent spasm of anti-Jewish hatred in America. If you are among those who marched in the streets chanting "Death to the Jews," or "Death to Israel," please stop. Those of you who intimidated your fellow Americans because they were Jewish—stop. You will not succeed. No matter how just you believe your cause to be, you are on the wrong side of this struggle. Please, for your own sake—for your own prosperity, your physical and mental well-being—stop.

No empire that has stood against the Jewish people has endured for long. Babylon lies in ruins; the bricks of her cities lie scattered. All we have of her history and culture is scratched into ceramic bricks that reside in museums. All that remains of ancient Rome are a few structures, mostly skeletal ruins. What remains of Nazi Germany is mostly on old film reels. The Soviet Union lasted barely 70 years. Egypt is a pathetic shadow of its former self. Libya is a failed state. Syria has been taken over by terrorists. Iraq is a puppet of its neighbor Iran. Iran, a current enemy of Israel, will eventually collapse as well if they do not make peace.

The modern enemies of Israel and the Jewish people have met with ignominious ends. Hitler bit into a cyanide capsule, shot himself, and was cremated outside his underground bunker. This was a fitting end for a man who gassed, shot, and cremated so many Jews.

Gamal Abdel Nasser, the president of Egypt from 1956 to 1970, was one of Israel's bitterest enemies. He was once hailed as a modern leader who could unite the Arab peoples. During his lifetime and tenure as president, Egypt attacked Israel multiple times. Nasser's armies were thoroughly defeated in humiliating fashion; the leader of Pan-Arab nationalism lived long enough to see his ideas disintegrate. Eventually, he died at a relatively young age.

Saddam Hussein was pulled out of a hole in the ground and hanged. Al Baghdadi was captured in an underground tunnel, and attacked by dogs, dying shortly thereafter. Muammar Qaddafi was pulled out of a hole in the ground and sodomized with knives and swords. In the end, all of these men met humiliating deaths.

Read the passage by Isaiah. It gives a sense of what is in store for the enemies of Israel.

> *All the kings of the nations, even all of them, lie in glory, every one in his own house. But thou art cast out of thy grave like an abominable branch, and as the raiment of those that are slain, thrust through with a sword, that go down to the stones of the pit; as a carcase trodden under feet. Thou shalt not be joined with them in burial, because thou hast destroyed thy land, and slain thy people: the seed of evildoers shall never be renowned. Prepare slaughter for his children for the iniquity of their fathers; that they do not rise, nor possess the land, nor fill the face of the world with cities. Isaiah 14:18-21*

This passage is written as a curse against the king of Babylon, who is equated with the fallen angel Lucifer. Hatred of the Jews is demonic. The metaphors of prophecy have manifested themselves literally in the lives of these men who fell from such heights.

As to the Church Replacing Israel in Prophecy

For those Christians who interpret the Old Testament prophecies about Israel as referring to the Church in general, or one specific denomination, it is clear this view is mistaken. I am not a theologian or a seminary professor, but I think you would be better off reading scripture with a more literal mindset. 'Israel' means Israel, just as 'God' means God, and 'eternal life' means eternal life.

Final Note to the Reader

If you do decide to begin reading the Bible with a greater sense of curiosity and faithfulness, you will not regret it. I've never known anyone who really read the Bible deeply who didn't feel richer for the experience. If you try to obey what you find inside the Bible, I think you will find the experience rewarding; the ride may get a little bumpy, though.

Buckle up, enjoy the ride.

Appendix I

The Declaration of the Establishment of the State of Israel

This entire text of the Declaration, translated into English, was taken from the Israeli Government's Ministry of Foreign Affairs Website.[160]

ERETZ-ISRAEL [(Hebrew) - the Land of Israel, Palestine] was the birthplace of the Jewish people. Here their spiritual, religious and political identity was shaped. Here they first attained to statehood, created cultural values of national and universal significance and gave to the world the eternal Book of Books.

After being forcibly exiled from their land, the people kept faith with it throughout their Dispersion and never ceased to pray and hope for their return to it and for the restoration in it of their political freedom. Impelled by this historic and traditional attachment, Jews strove in every successive generation to re-establish themselves in their ancient homeland. In recent decades they returned in their masses. Pioneers, ma'pilim [(Hebrew) - immigrants coming to Eretz-Israel in defiance of restrictive legislation] and defenders, they made deserts bloom, revived the Hebrew language, built villages and towns, and created a thriving community controlling its own economy and culture, loving peace but knowing how to defend itself, bringing the blessings of progress to all the country's inhabitants, and aspiring towards independent nationhood.

In the year 5657 (1897), at the summons of the spiritual father of the Jewish State, Theodore Herzl, the First Zionist Congress convened and proclaimed the right of the Jewish people to national rebirth in its own country.

This right was recognized in the Balfour Declaration of the 2nd November, 1917, and re-affirmed in the Mandate of the League of Nations which, in particular, gave international sanction to the historic connection between the Jewish people and Eretz-Israel and to the right of the Jewish people to rebuild its National Home.

---

[160] "The Declaration of the Establishment of the State of Israel." 2024. Israel Ministry of Foreign Affairs. www.gov.il. Accessed April 10, 2025. https://www.gov.il/en/pages/declaration-of-establishment-state-of-israel.

The catastrophe which recently befell the Jewish people - the massacre of millions of Jews in Europe - was another clear demonstration of the urgency of solving the problem of its homelessness by re-establishing in Eretz-Israel the Jewish State, which would open the gates of the homeland wide to every Jew and confer upon the Jewish people the status of a fully privileged member of the comity of nations.

Survivors of the Nazi holocaust in Europe, as well as Jews from other parts of the world, continued to migrate to Eretz-Israel, undaunted by difficulties, restrictions and dangers, and never ceased to assert their right to a life of dignity, freedom and honest toil in their national homeland.

In the Second World War, the Jewish community of this country contributed its full share to the struggle of the freedom- and peace-loving nations against the forces of Nazi wickedness and, by the blood of its soldiers and its war effort, gained the right to be reckoned among the peoples who founded the United Nations.

On the 29th November, 1947, the United Nations General Assembly passed a resolution calling for the establishment of a Jewish State in Eretz-Israel; the General Assembly required the inhabitants of Eretz-Israel to take such steps as were necessary on their part for the implementation of that resolution. This recognition by the United Nations of the right of the Jewish people to establish their State is irrevocable.

This right is the natural right of the Jewish people to be masters of their own fate, like all other nations, in their own sovereign State.

ACCORDINGLY WE, MEMBERS OF THE PEOPLE'S COUNCIL, REPRESENTATIVES OF THE JEWISH COMMUNITY OF ERETZ-ISRAEL AND OF THE ZIONIST MOVEMENT, ARE HERE ASSEMBLED ON THE DAY OF THE TERMINATION OF THE BRITISH MANDATE OVER ERETZ-ISRAEL AND, BY VIRTUE OF OUR NATURAL AND HISTORIC RIGHT AND ON THE STRENGTH OF THE RESOLUTION OF THE UNITED NATIONS GENERAL ASSEMBLY, HEREBY DECLARE THE ESTABLISHMENT OF A JEWISH STATE IN ERETZ-ISRAEL, TO BE KNOWN AS THE STATE OF ISRAEL.

WE DECLARE that, with effect from the moment of the termination of the Mandate being tonight, the eve of Sabbath, the 6th Iyar, 5708 (15th May, 1948), until the establishment of the elected, regular authorities of the State in accordance with the Constitution which shall be adopted by the Elected Constituent Assembly not later than the 1st October 1948, the People's Council shall act as a Provisional Council of State, and its executive organ, the People's Administration, shall be the Provisional Government of the Jewish State, to be called "Israel".

THE STATE OF ISRAEL will be open for Jewish immigration and for the Ingathering of the Exiles; it will foster the development of the country for the benefit of all its inhabitants; it will be based on freedom, justice and peace as envisaged by the prophets of Israel; it will ensure complete equality of social and political rights to all its inhabitants irrespective of religion, race or sex; it will guarantee freedom of religion, conscience, language, education and culture; it will safeguard the Holy Places of all religions; and it will be faithful to the principles of the Charter of the United Nations.

THE STATE OF ISRAEL is prepared to cooperate with the agencies and representatives of the United Nations in implementing the resolution of the General Assembly of the 29th November, 1947, and will take steps to bring about the economic union of the whole of Eretz-Israel.

WE APPEAL to the United Nations to assist the Jewish people in the building-up of its State and to receive the State of Israel into the comity of nations.

WE APPEAL - in the very midst of the onslaught launched against us now for months - to the Arab inhabitants of the State of Israel to preserve peace and participate in the upbuilding of the State on the basis of full and equal citizenship and due representation in all its provisional and permanent institutions.

WE EXTEND our hand to all neighbouring states and their peoples in an offer of peace and good neighbourliness, and appeal to them to establish bonds of cooperation and mutual help with the sovereign Jewish people settled in its own land. The State of Israel is prepared to do its share in a common effort for the advancement of the entire Middle East.

WE APPEAL to the Jewish people throughout the Diaspora to rally round the Jews of Eretz-Israel in the tasks of immigration and upbuilding and to stand by them in the great struggle for the realization of the age-old dream - the redemption of Israel.

PLACING OUR TRUST IN THE "ROCK OF ISRAEL", WE AFFIX OUR SIGNATURES TO THIS PROCLAMATION AT THIS SESSION OF THE PROVISIONAL COUNCIL OF STATE, ON THE SOIL OF THE HOMELAND, IN THE CITY OF TEL-AVIV, ON THIS SABBATH EVE, THE 5TH DAY OF IYAR, 5708 (14TH MAY,1948).[161]

---

[161] "The Declaration of the Establishment of the State of Israel." 2024. Israel Ministry of Foreign Affairs. www.gov.il. 2024. Accessed April 10, 2025. https://www.gov.il/en/pages/declaration-of-establishment-state-of-israel.

Appendix II

Full Text of Balfour Letter[162]

Foreign Office
November 2nd, 1917

Dear Lord Rothschild,

I have much pleasure in conveying to you, on behalf of this Majesty's Government, the following declaration of sympathy with Jewish Zionist aspirations which has been submitted to, and approved by, the Cabinet.

"His Majesty's Government view with favour the establishment in Palestine of a national home for the Jewish people, and will use their best endeavors to facilitate the achievement of this object, it being clearly understood that nothing shall be done which may prejudice the civil and religious rights of existing non-Jewish communities in Palestine, or the rights and political status enjoyed by Jews in any other country."

I should be grateful if you would bring this declaration to the knowledge of the Zionist Federation.

Yours sincerely,

Arthur James Balfour

---

[162] My Jewish Learning. 2009. "The Balfour Declaration Full Text." My Jewish Learning. Accessed April 10, 2025.
https://www.myjewishlearning.com/article/read-the-balfour-declaration/.

Appendix III
Daniel 5 Numbers Analysis

Daniel 5, by the Numbers

The following four or five pages contain a specific breakdown of the noun frequency values for Daniel 5. The word 'thousand,' is equated to its numerical value, not its frequency in the chapter. In the original Aramaic, Daniel 5 ends with verse 5:30. As a result, the Aramaic word *malkut* meaning, "kingdom" or "reign," only occurs nine times and holds the value of nine in this analysis. The Aramaic word *enesh* in English "man" or "whosoever"(Daniel 5:7) is a common noun in Aramaic and holds the value four.

The noun frequency values add up to 2,520 at Daniel 5:9, when the queen enters the banquet. Daniel arranged the nouns surrounding verse nine and ten so that the number 2484 can be found when those nouns are multiplied. In other words, Daniel arranged these nouns so that they would have a numerical significance whether added or multiplied.

Observe the verse-by-verse breakdown of noun frequency values below:

Chapter Five Word Frequency Analysis

Noun	Number of Occurrences	
5:1		
Belshazzar	6	
king	23	
feast	1	
thousand	1000	
lords	6	
wine	4	
thousand	1000	
	Total	**2040**
5:2		
Belshazzar	6	
wine	4	

gold	7
silver	3
vessels	3
father	6
Nebuchadnezzar	3
Temple	3
Jerusalem	2
King	23
Princes	6
Wives	3
Concubines	3
	Total 72

5:3

golden	7
vessels	3
temple	3
house	3
God	10
Jerusalem	2
king	23
princes	6
wives	3
concubines	3
	Total 63

5:4

Wine	4
Gods	10
Gold	7
Silver	3
brass,	2
iron,	2
wood	2
stone.	2
	Total 32

5:5

Hour	1
fingers	1
man's	4
hand	4
candlestick	1

plaister	1
wall	1
king	23
palace:	3
king	23
part	2
hand	3
	Total 67

5:6

king	23
countenance	3
thoughts	2
joints	3
loins	1
knees	1
	Total 33

5:7

King	23
astrologers	3
Chaldeans	3
Soothsayers	2
king	23
wise men	3
Babylon	1
Whosoever (Aramaic 'enesh' Strong's H606)	4
Writing	7
Interpretation	10
scarlet	3
chain	3
gold	7
neck	3
third	3
ruler	2
kingdom.	9
	Total 109

5:8

King	23	
wise men	3	
writing	7	
king	23	
interpretation	10	
	Total	**66**

5:9

king	23	
Belshazzar	6	
Countenance	3	2,484
Lords	6	
	Total	**38**

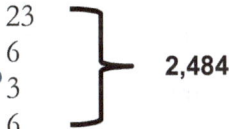

Multiplied together equal 2,484

Grand Total Verse 5:1-9   **2,520**

The noun frequency values for Daniel 5:1-9 add up to 2,520. The last four noun values in Daniel 5:9, when multiplied, equal 2,484.

If we look at the next thirteen nouns in Daniel 5:10-11, we see two more times that the values can be multiplied to equal 2,484.

Daniel 5:10

Queen	2	
Words	3	
King	23	2,484
Lords	6	
banquet	1	
house	3	
queen	2	
king	23	
for ever	1	
thoughts	2	2,484
countenance	3	

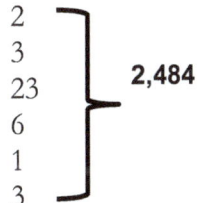

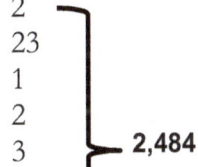

Multiplied together equal 2,484

Multiplied together equal 2,484

5:11

man	1	
kingdom	9	

Verses nine, ten and eleven have at least three equations embedded in the text that give the product of 2,484. The combined sum of the nouns from verse one through verse nine is 2,520. This is very strong circumstantial evidence that Daniel intended the reader to understand 2,484 equates to 2,520 in some way.

The most obvious way to understand this is as a timeline. The ratio of 2,484 to 2,520 equals 69 to 70 exactly. The math is simple; the largest common denominator of 2,484 and 2,520 is 36. The number 2,484 is 36*69; the number 2520 is 36*70. Daniel uses the ratio 69 to 70 in the ninth chapter with the so-called 70 weeks prophecy, so this is no accident. This is time related.

When we multiply 2,520 years of 360 days each, we get 907,200 days. So, how many solar years is this? Divide 907,200 days by a solar year of 365.242 days and we get 2483.83 years. This is very close to 2,484. The ratio of 360 days to 365.242 days is very close to the ratio of 69 to 70.

Daniel embedded timelines in Daniel 5. In other chapters, Daniel used solar years and 360-day years or 'times.' In Daniel 5 he intended the 360-day 'time' to be used; 2,520 'times' is 907,200 days.

Appendix IV

Babylonian Number Systems

Base-60 and Babylonian Numbers

According to the first chapter of Daniel, Daniel and his friends received a Babylonian education in order to serve the king.[163] It is probably safe to assume that, as a part of this training, Daniel received some level of indoctrination in the Babylonian system of mathematics.

Ancient Babylon's numbers were based on the number 60. This base-60, or sexagesimal system, was passed down to the Babylonians from ancient Sumeria and had been in use for 2,000 years by the time Daniel arrived in Babylon.[164] Sexagesimal is the proper name for this number system; for the sake of clarity and simplicity, I use the term base-60.

Our number system, the decimal system, relies on base ten. In our system, we use nine written symbols to represent the natural numbers one through nine. We have a tenth symbol, zero, representing the absence of value. These numbers are organized in columns, each representing factors of ten. The first column represents units, the next column represents tens, then hundreds, and so on, advancing by factors of ten. For example, the number 2,520 is made up of two thousands, five hundreds, two tens, and zero units. This is the system familiar to most Westerners.[165]

By comparison, ancient Babylon used a roughly decimal system to represent the values of one through fifty-nine, with columns to represent values larger than fifty-nine. These columns advanced by

---

[163] Daniel 1:4,17,20

[164] History of Math and Technology. 2024. "The Babylonian Number System - History of Math and Technology." February 28, 2024. Accessed April 11, 2025. https://www.historymath.com/the-babylonian-number-system/.

[165] History of Math and Technology. 2024. "The Babylonian Number System - History of Math and Technology." February 28, 2024. Accessed April 11, 2025. https://www.historymath.com/the-babylonian-number-system/.

factors of 60. For example, there was a units column, a 60s column, a 3600s column, and so on, each advancing by factors of 60.

The ancient Babylonians used wedges to represent numbers. In the Babylonian system, vertical wedges represented units, or 'ones,' and horizontal wedges represented 'tens.' Two horizontal wedges placed next to five vertical wedges could represent the number 25. However, the Babylonians did not use markers to indicate which factor of 60 was represented. As a result, that same arrangement could represent 25 in the 60s column or 1,500. They relied heavily on context to resolve such ambiguities.

Before we go any further into this, observe the chart below to get a visual representation of these wedges. You will notice that the number of vertical wedges represents the value of units; the number of horizontal wedges represents the numerical value in tens.

166167

The Babylonian Number System—no zero, no placeholder

Our number system uses zero to represent the absence of value. In the example of 2,520, the zero in the units column signifies the absence of value in that column. In this way, zero serves as a sort of placeholder. The number to the left, '2,' represents the total in the

---

166 This chart is available on multiple sites online. I don't know who published it first. The earliest rendition I found was on Pinterest 2017, by James Nickel.

167 Nickel, James. 2017. "Beauty of Mathematics." Pinterest. August 7, 2017. Accessed April 10, 2025. https://www.pinterest.com/pin/556898310164694933/.

'tens' column because the zero acts as a placeholder in the units column.

There is very little ambiguity in our system, though our system is not perfect. We have difficulty expressing precise ratios if the numbers do not easily convert to factors of ten. Nevertheless, this lack of ambiguity in our numbers provides a great deal of stability.

The ancient Babylonians had no concept to represent the absence of value—they had no zero. They relied heavily on context to determine whether a written number represented values in the units column, 60s, or 3600s column.[168]

Using the number 2,520 as our example, in base-60 we would express this as $42,0_{base60}$. This indicates that there are 42 sixties and no units. However, the ancient Babylonians had no placeholder. In that case, the number 2,520 would simply be written as 42. Readers would have to rely on context to understand whether 42 indicates 42 units, 42 sixties (2,520) or 42 3600s (151,200). As a result, the number 42 was virtually indistinguishable from 2,520 or 151,200.

The Babylonian system used cuneiform writing (wedge-shaped symbols), the number 42 was represented by four horizontal wedges (representing four tens) and two vertical wedges ⫶𝖙. You can confirm this in the previous chart. In base-60 we would express 2,520 as $42,0_{base60}$; the number 151,200 would be $42,0,0_{base60}$. The Babylonians during Daniel's lifetime, simply wrote ⫶𝖙 and relied on context to sort out ambiguities as to whether this represented 42 units, 42 sixties, or some other factor of 60.

This ambiguity is confusing to a modern Western eye. The Babylonians apparently did not have any problems with this.

If you take a look at the table below you will see how various values could be represented using very similar or identical symbols.

---

[168] History of Math and Technology. 2024. "The Babylonian Number System - History of Math and Technology." February 28, 2024. Accessed April 11, 2025. https://www.historymath.com/the-babylonian-number-system/.

Base 10 Decimal	Base-60 Sexagesimal	6th Cent. BC Babylonian	3rd Cent. BC Babylonian
42	42_{base60}		[cuneiform]
2,520	$42,0_{base60}$	[cuneiform]	[cuneiform]
151,200	$42,0,0_{base60}$		[cuneiform]
252	$4,12_{base60}$		[cuneiform]
15,120	$4,12,0_{base60}$	[cuneiform]	[cuneiform]
907,200	$4,12,0,0_{base60}$		[cuneiform]

By the 3rd century BC, the Babylonians developed a placeholder to indicate whether a number belonged in the units, 60s, or 3,600s column. That symbol consisted of two wedges canted at an angle. However, in Daniel's lifetime, this symbol was not yet in use.

Daniel apparently used this ambiguity to his advantage. Not every embedded equation resulted in 2,520 or 907,200; some of the equations reflected their Babylonian base-60 equivalents.

Part of the reason interpreters missed these equations is that we approach numbers from a base-10 perspective.

Bibliography

"Babylonian Cuneiform Numerals." Wikipedia. Last Modified April 2, 2025. Accessed April 10, 2025. https://en.wikipedia.org/wiki/Babylonian_cuneiform_numerals.

"Babylonian Numerals Converter - Online Number System Calculator." 2015. Dcode.fr. Accessed April 10, 2025. https://www.dcode.fr/babylonian-numbers.

"How the Modern State of Israel Was Created in 1948." n.d. History Skills. Accessed April 10, 2025. https://www.historyskills.com/classroom/modern-history/formation-of-modern-israel-reading/.

"Julian Day and Date Time Calculator." n.d. www.csgnetwork.com. Accessed April 11, 2025. http://www.csgnetwork.com/juliandaydate.html.

"Steganography | Definition of Steganography by Webster's Online Dictionary." 2025. Webster-Dictionary.org. Accessed April 11, 2025. https://www.webster-dictionary.org/definition/Steganography.

"The Declaration of the Establishment of the State of Israel." 2024. Israel Ministry of Foreign Affairs. www.gov.il. Accessed April 10, 2025. https://www.gov.il/en/pages/declaration-of-establishment-state-of-israel.

"The Palestine Campaign: How Britain Captured Jerusalem in World War One." History Hit. December 6, 2018. Accessed April 11, 2025. https://www.historyhit.com/1917-general-allenby-enters-jerusalem/

"What Do the Words Mene, Mene, Tekel, Upharsin Mean (Daniel 5:25)?" n.d. www.cgg.org. Accessed November 2, 2022. https://www.cgg.org/index.cfm/library/bqa/id/65/what-do-words-mene-mene-tekel-upharsin-mean-daniel-525.htm.

Avineri, Shlomo. 2013. *Herzl*. Hachette UK.

Bar-Am, Aviva. 2012. "In the Footsteps of Wilhelm II." The Jerusalem Post | JPost.com. *The Jerusalem Post.* November 29, 2012. Accessed April 10, 2025. https://www.jpost.com/In-Jerusalem/Features/In-the-footsteps-of-Wilhelm-II.

Barker, Kenneth L, and Donald W Burdick. 1995. *The NIV Study Bible.* Grand Rapids, Mi: Zondervan Pub. House.

Barker, Kenneth L., and John R. Kohlenberger. 1994. *Zondervan NIV Bible Commentary, vol. 1: Old Testament.* Grand Rapids, Mich: Zondervan.

Ben-Gurion, David. 2019. "Theodor Herzl | Austrian Zionist Leader." *Encyclopedia Britannica.* Last modified March 2, 2025. Accessed April 10, 2025. https://www.britannica.com/biography/Theodor-Herzl.

Blue Letter Bible. 2019. "Bible Search and Study Tools - Blue Letter Bible." BlueletterBible.org. Blue Letter Bible. 2019. Accessed April 11, 2025. https://www.blueletterBible.org/.

Brack-Bernsen, Lis. n.d. "The 360-Day Year in Mesopotamia." Accessed March 25, 2025. https://epub.uni-regensburg.de/58013/1/31.the%20360%20day%20year.pdf.

Bradsher, Greg. 2010. "The Nuremberg Laws." *Prologue Magazine.* 2010. Last updated April 2023. Accessed April 10, 2025. The U.S. National Archives and Records Administration. https://www.archives.gov/publications/prologue/2010/winter/nuremberg.html.

Breedlove, Robert. 2022. "The Number Zero and Bitcoin." Medium. June 24, 2022. https://breedlove22.medium.com/the-number-zero-and-bitcoin-4c193336db5b.

Brice, William Charles and Walid Ahmed Khalidi. n.d. "Palestine - the Arab Revolt." *Encyclopedia Britannica.* Accessed April 10, 2025. https://www.britannica.com/place/Palestine/The-Arab-Revolt.

Britannica editors. 1998. "Egyptian Calendar, Dating System." *Encyclopedia Britannica*. Last modified June 8, 2017. Accessed April 10, 2025. https://www.britannica.com/science/Egyptian-calendar#ref1248450

Britannica editors. 2025. "Balfour Declaration | History & Impact." *Encyclopedia Britannica*. Accessed April 10, 2025. https://www.britannica.com/event/Balfour-Declaration.

Britannica editors. 2025. "United Nations Resolution 181 | Map & Summary." *Encyclopedia Britannica*. Accessed April 10, 2025. https://www.britannica.com/topic/United-Nations-Resolution-181.

Britannica editors. 2025. "Tyre." *Encyclopedia Britannica*. Last modified January 9, 2025. Accessed April 10, 2025. https://www.britannica.com/place/Tyre.

Center for Israeli Education. Editorial Staff. 2023. "Herzl's Body Buried in Israel | CIE." CIE. August 17, 2023. April 11, 2025. https://israeled.org/herzls-body-buried-in-israel/.

Dixon, Helen. 2022. "Reexamining Nebuchadnezzar II's 'Thirteen-Year' Siege of Tyre in Phoenician Historiography." *Journal of Ancient History 10 (2): 165–99*. Accessed April 11, 2025. https://doi.org/10.1515/jah-2022-0007.

Engelmayer, Jay. 2022. "The Balfour Declaration & the Mandate for Palestine - 1917 - 1922." *The Judean*. May 23, 2022. Accessed April 10, 2025. https://thejudean.com/index.php/history/64-the-balfour-declaration-the-mandate-for-palestine-1917-1922.

Ettinger, Shmuel. n.d. "The Balfour Declaration of 1917." Reprinted by My Jewish Learning. Accessed April 11, 2025. https://www.myjewishlearning.com/article/the-balfour-declaration/

Facing History & Ourselves. 2016. "The Persistence of Antisemitism | Facing History and Ourselves." www.facinghistory.org. August 2, 2016. Accessed April 10,2025. https://www.facinghistory.org/resource-library/persistence-antisemitism.

Flaws, Jacob. 2025. "The Nuremberg Race Laws." The National WWII Museum | New Orleans. Last modified January 7, 2025. Accessed April 10, 2025. https://www.nationalww2museum.org/war/articles/nuremberg-laws.

Gaebelein, Arno Clemens. 1911. *The Prophet Daniel. A Key to the Visions and Prophecies of the Book of Daniel.* Second Edition. London; New York Printed: Marshall Bros. Kindle.

Gjevori, Elis. "How Theodor Herzl Failed to Convince the Ottomans to Sell Palestine." n.d. Accessed April 9, 2025. *TRTWorld.* https://www.trtworld.com/magazine/how-theodor-herzl-failed-to-convince-the-ottomans-to-sell-palestine-46991.

Gross, Rachel E. 2018. "Kielce: The Post-Holocaust Pogrom That Poland Is Still Fighting Over." *Smithsonian.* Smithsonian.com. January 8, 2018. Accessed April 10, 2025. https://www.smithsonianmag.com/history/kielce-post-holocaust-pogrom-poland-still-fighting-over-180967681/.

Guzik, David. 2022. "Study Guide for Jeremiah 32." Blue Letter Bible. June 16, 2022. Accessed April 10, 2025. https://www.blueletterBible.org/comm/guzik_david/study-guide/jeremiah/jeremiah-32.cfm

HebCal. n.d. "Jewish Calendar 1918 Diaspora - Hebcal." Hebcal.com. Accessed April 11, 2025. https://www.hebcal.com/hebcal?year=1918&v=1&yt=G&nx=on&D=on&d=on&c=off&maj=on&min=on&mod=on&mf=on&ss=on.

HebCal. n.d. "Jewish Calendar 1947 Diaspora - Hebcal."
Hebcal.com. Accessed April 11, 2025.
https://www.hebcal.com/hebcal?year=1947&v=1&yt=G&n
x=on&o=on&d=on&c=off&maj=on&min=on&mod=on&
mf=off&ss=off.

History of Math and Technology. 2024. "The Babylonian Number
System - History of Math and Technology." February 28,
2024. Accessed April 11, 2025.
https://www.historymath.com/the-babylonian-number-
system/.

Horowitz, Wayne. 1996. "The 360- and 364-Day Year in Ancient
Mesopotamia." *Journal of the Ancient Near Eastern Society 24 (1)*.
Accessed April 11, 2025.
https://www.academia.edu/74071999/The_360_and_364_d
ay_year_in_ancient_Mesopotamia.

Jewish Encyclopedia. n.d. "GO'EL." Accessed April 11, 2025.
https://www.jewishencyclopedia.com/articles/6734-go-el.

Jewish Virtual Library. 2015. "Theodor (Binyamin Ze'ev) Herzl."
Accessed April 10, 2025.
https://www.jewishvirtuallibrary.org/theodor-binyamin-ze-
rsquo-ev-herzl.

Jewish Virtual Library. 2019. "Estimated Number of Jews Killed in
the Final Solution." Jewishvirtuallibrary.org. 2019. Accessed
April 10, 2025.
https://www.jewishvirtuallibrary.org/estimated-number-of-
jews-killed-in-the-final-solution.

Jewish Virtual Library. n.d. "UN General Assembly Resolution 181."
www.jewishvirtuallibrary.org. Accessed April 10, 2025.
https://www.jewishvirtuallibrary.org/un-general-assembly-
resolution-181-2.

Jewish Virtual Library. n.d."Turks Surrender Jerusalem to the
British." Accessed April 11, 2025.
https://www.jewishvirtuallibrary.org/general-edmond-
allenby-marches-into-jerusalem.

Jones, Arnold Hugh Martin and Kathleen Mary Kenyon. 1999. "Palestine - the Arab Revolt." Encyclopedia Britannica. Last modified October 15, 2024. Accessed April 9, 2025. https://www.britannica.com/place/Palestine/The-Arab-Revolt.

Karsh, Efraim. 2008. *The Arab-Israeli Conflict: The 1948 War.* New York: Rosen Pub. Kindle Edition.

Lakoff, George, and Mark Johnson. 2008. *Metaphors We Live By.* Chicago: University of Chicago Press.

Lester, Mike. 2024. *2520: The Hidden Key in the Book of Daniel.* First. Independently Published.

Muhammed, Shukir. 2016. "Brick Stamped with the Name of Nebuchadnezzar II." *World History Encyclopedia.* June 17, 2016. Accessed April 11, 2025. https://www.worldhistory.org/image/5240/brick-stamped-with-the-name-of-nebuchadnezzar-ii/.

My Jewish Learning. 2009. "The Balfour Declaration Full Text." My Jewish Learning. Accessed April 10, 2025. https://www.myjewishlearning.com/article/read-the-balfour-declaration/.

My Jewish Learning. 2017. "A Timeline of the Holocaust." My Jewish Learning. Accessed April 9, 2025. https://www.myjewishlearning.com/article/a-timeline-of-the-holocaust/.

Newport, Frank. 2022. "Fewer in U.S. Now See Bible as Literal Word of God." Gallup.com. July 6, 2022. Accessed March 1, 2025. https://news.gallup.com/poll/394262/fewer-Bible-literal-word-god.aspx.

Nickel, James. 2017. "Beauty of Mathematics." Pinterest. August 7, 2017. Accessed April 10, 2025. https://www.pinterest.com/pin/556898310164694933/.

Parker, Richard A, and Waldo H Dubberstein. 2007. *Babylonian Chronology 626 B.C.- A.D. 75*. Eugene, Or.: Wipf & Stock.

Payne, J Barton. 1973. *Encyclopedia of Biblical Prophecy: The Complete Guide to Scriptural Predictions and Their Fulfillment*. New York: Harper & Row.

Radner, Karen and Grant Frame. 2020. *THE ROYAL INSCRIPTIONS OF AMĒL-MARDUK (561–560 BC), NERIGLISSAR (559–556 BC), AND NABONIDUS (555–539 BC), KINGS OF BABYLON: THE ROYAL INSCRIPTIONS OF THE NEO-BABYLONIAN EMPIRE*. University Park, Pennsylvania. Pennsylvania State University.

Rambsel, Yacov A. 2000. *The Genesis Factor: The Amazing Mysteries of the Bible Codes*. Beverly Hills, Ca: Lion's Head Pub.

Ray, Michael. 2019. "Julian Calendar | History & Difference from Gregorian Calendar." *Encyclopedia Britannica*. Last modified December 2024. Accessed April 10, 2025. https://www.britannica.com/science/Julian-calendar.

Safran, Nadav. 1982. *Israel—the Embattled Ally*. Harvard University Press.

Saggs, H.W. 2000. "Babylon." *Encyclopedia Britannica*. Last modified March 18, 2025. Accessed April 10, 2025. https://www.britannica.com/place/Babylon-ancient-city-Mesopotamia-Asia.

Sefaria. 2023. "Jeremiah 32:44." Accessed April 11, 2025. https://www.sefaria.org/Jeremiah.32.44?lang=b.

Space Awareness. "Counting and Reading the Hour in Cuneiform Digits." Accessed April 11, 2025. https://www.space-awareness.org/bg/activities/6053/counting-and-reading-the-hour-in-cuneiform-digits/.

Thiele, Edwin R. 2004. *The Mysterious Numbers of the Hebrew Kings.* Grand Rapids, Mi: Kregel.

Underwood, Alice E.M. n.d. "What Is a Metaphor? —Definition and Examples | Grammarly." Last modified February 18, 2025. Accessed April 9, 2025. https://www.grammarly.com/blog/literary-devices/metaphor/?msockid=3990126e2b83659a095207d62a946454.

United Nations. 1947. "Palestine Plan of Partition with Economic Union - General Assembly Resolution 181." Un.org. Question of Palestine. Document is dated 1947, no info available on website creation date. Accessed April 11, 2025. https://www.un.org/unispal/document/auto-insert-185393/.

United States Holocaust Memorial Museum. n.d. "Nazi Territorial Aggression: The Anschluss." Holocaust Encyclopedia. Accessed April 10, 2025. https://encyclopedia.ushmm.org/content/en/article/nazi-territorial-aggression-the-anschluss.

United States Holocaust Memorial Museum. 2019. "The Wannsee Conference and the 'Final Solution.'" Ushmm.org. Last modified December 8, 2020. Accessed April 10, 2025. https://encyclopedia.ushmm.org/content/en/article/the-wannsee-conference-and-the-final-solution.

United States Holocaust Memorial Museum. 2024. "Timeline of Events." Holocaust encyclopedia. Accessed April 9, 2025. https://encyclopedia.ushmm.org/content/en/timeline/holocaust.

Vashem, Yad. 2019. "Murder of the Jews of Poland | www.yadvashem.org." Yadvashem.org. 2019. Accessed April 10, 2025. https://www.yadvashem.org/holocaust/about/fate-of-jews/poland.html.

Walvoord, John F. 2011. *Every Prophecy of the Bible: Clear Explanations for Uncertain Times.* Colorado Springs, Co: David C. Cook.

Wasserstein, Bernard. 2011. "BBC - History - World Wars: European Refugee Movements after World War Two." www.bbc.co.uk. February 17, 2011. Accessed April 10, 2025. https://www.bbc.co.uk/history/worldwars/wwtwo/refugees _01.shtml.

Weiner, Rebecca and Mitchell Ward. 2013. "Poland Virtual Jewish History Tour." Jewishvirtuallibrary.org. Last modified January 29, 2025. Accessed April 10, 2025. https://www.jewishvirtuallibrary.org/poland-virtual-jewish-history-tour.

Windle, Bryan. 2019. "Nebuchadnezzar: An Archaeological Biography." *Bible Archaeology Report*. October 17, 2019. Accessed April 10, 2025. https://Biblearchaeologyreport.com/2019/10/17/nebuchad nezzar-an-archaeological-biography/.

Windle, Bryan. 2022. "Hophra: An Archaeological Biography." *Bible Archaeology Report*. February 4, 2022. Accessed April 10, 2025. https://biblearchaeologyreport.com/2022/02/04/hophra-an-archaeological-biography/.